From Liz

17

G000079427

These
Circuses
That Sweep Through the
Landscape

These Circuses That Sweep Through the Landscape

· stories ·

Tejaswini Apte-Rahm

ALEPH

ALEPH

ALEPH BOOK COMPANY
An independent publishing firm
promoted by *Rupa Publications India*

First published in India in 2017 by
Aleph Book Company
7/16 Ansari Road, Daryaganj
New Delhi 110 002

'Homo Coleoptera' first appeared in the January
2000 issue of *HIMAL Southasian* magazine.
'Sandalwood' first appeared in *BLink*'s fiction issue,
January 2016.

ISBN: 978-93-84067-56-4

1 3 5 7 9 10 8 6 4 2

Printed and bound in India by Replika Press Pvt. Ltd.

For Arvind and Suneeti, my parents

Contents

Homo Coleoptera

Apart from his beetle collection, most of Mr Ghosh's prized possessions had been won in contests. Early on in life, he realized that all he had to do, once he had filled in the form and cut along the dotted line, was send in his entry and then simply will the prizes his way. When it came to contests, he had the willpower of a bull. Nine times out of ten it worked. He had paid off more than half his loans with prize money saved over the years. The bank job paid for the other half. His second car had magically arrived at his doorstep one morning, some weeks after he had filled in a multiple choice questionnaire about a new brand of milk chocolate, and completed a slogan that said, 'Milky Munchy Mints are the best because milk is for health and mint is for taste.' It wouldn't have mattered much had Mr Ghosh written, 'Because they come in real handy when you want to throw up.' He would have won the blue Santro anyway. Simply because he had willed it to happen.

In fact, Mr Ghosh was sure, as he rubbed his clean-shaven chin with thin, artistic fingers, if most of the really good contests weren't rigged to benefit some distant relation of the managing director, he'd have been a millionaire by now and would have travelled the globe twice over on airline-ticket prizes. Had he travelled the globe thus, thought Mr Ghosh dreamily, ensconced in his red armchair with *The Further Expanded Beetle Encyclopaedia* (opened at S—*Scarabaeoidea*) on his lap, he would have been able to obtain the predaceous great diving beetle, *Dytiscus marginalis*, from northern Asia. He would have hunted for one of the five species of *Amphizoidae* in Alaska. And he wouldn't have had to order the enormous, shiny, four-inch long African Goliath from the Coleoptera Collectors' Society. What a beauty it was! He might have come upon it himself, crawling through the quiet, leafy undergrowth of an African jungle. The Initial Sighting. The Stalk. The Inching Closer. A sudden, strong splutter of wings and six crawly legs frantically pawing at the still, humid air. And the giant would be his. This was an unlikely fantasy, since Mr Ghosh, even if he had been able to afford it, had neither the pluck nor the endurance to go on any such expedition.

However, his years as a banker had produced in him the particular temperament (or perhaps it was the other way around) of a meticulous desktop researcher. And so Mr Ghosh's head was filled with practically everything there was to know about beetles, from their antennae ('usually eleven-segmented', he would clarify to anyone who cared to listen) to their mandibles ('often triangular in shape'), from their ten-segmented abdomens ('though all ten segments are not externally visible always') to the thin little hairs ('sometimes not so thin') on their legs.

He had a formidable collection of beetles entrapped for posterity in a variety of glass-topped trays in his desk. Painstakingly gathered over the years, the variously shaped and sized creatures lay spreadeagled on their abdomens, each with a long silver pin thinly piercing its exoskeleton, firmly fastening the shelly carcass to the soft green board underneath. Below each beetle was a neat white label detailing its taxonomic classification. Arranged in rows so that they all faced the same direction, they were like so many phalanxes arrayed for battle, frozen in a state of suspended animation, held as if by a magic spell which, when lifted, would send them all scuttling up the board like tanks or whirring out the window like helicopter gunships. Only the prized African Goliath was awarded a small, glass-covered tray of its very own, where it lay in armoured splendour, its crisp wings never losing their sheen.

In the silence of his curtained study, where the tall, thick columns of red velvet muffled every sound save the steady ticking of the wall clock, Mr Ghosh would pore over his tomes, then examine his collection, various facts, histories and explanations of beetle structure (physical and familial) turning over in his mind. Occasionally, he would remove the glass casing and thoughtfully nudge some of the less rare beetles with his pen. At other times he would just bend over other, more precious, specimens with a magnifying glass.

Mr Ghosh had another prized possession: often, he would call Mrs Ghosh his ladybird ('family *Coccinellidae*', he would remark, playfully). She was beautiful. And Mr Ghosh knew that, thanks to clever matchmaking by his parents, he had indeed been lucky. Mrs Ghosh's hair was silk-soft, thick and black. When she left it loose, it cascaded about her round, shapely buttocks. Her skin was luminous and creamy, her eyes large and shapely, as expressive as a Bharatanatyam danseuse. Her bare waist (which had about it just a hint of fat) showing through the folds of the diaphanous chiffon saris she was so fond of, would make Mr Ghosh's heart flutter like a moth. Her smile was sweet and wide, displaying pearly teeth. And she cooked the most delectable food he had ever tasted. Mrs Ghosh was perfect.

Except that she never seemed to understand her husband's passion for beetles. Soon after they were married, he had taken her eagerly by the hand to his desk and brought out his trays. She had flinched and shuddered as if the whole pack of them had come alive and scurried down her bare back.

But apart from her lack of appreciation of his collection, she had never denied Mr Ghosh anything. She supported him wholeheartedly, helping him concentrate on willing prizes to come his way. She cooked delicious meals for him day after day. She never withheld her beautiful body from him. She would give herself to him without a murmur, wrapping her shapely legs around his thin, bony hips, smiling up at him as he grunted out his pleasure. She never shied away when, looking up from his beetle collection, he felt a desire to touch a shapely breast as she bent over his desk with his evening tea tray.

And yet, despite all this, Mr Ghosh felt that she was withholding her essential being from him. And that made him furious. He felt that she could have wrapped her legs around him a little more tightly in bed. He thought that her smile could have been wider and more inviting when he returned home every evening. He knew her lips could have been more yielding to his kisses. Worst of all, he had seen a special smile and sparkle in her eyes whenever she met his cousin Amolan at family gatherings. A sparkle and smile that was never directed at Mr Ghosh. After the obligatory circuit of the room was over, Amolan and Mrs Ghosh would inevitably end up in a corner together, talking animatedly about God knows what, with Mrs Ghosh laughing at Amolan's pathetic little jokes till her sides ached. Mr Ghosh had tried joining them a couple of times, but felt excluded. Amolan and Mrs Ghosh talked about films and books he knew little about. They laughed at jokes which Mr Ghosh didn't find funny in the least.

And their eyes seemed to know he was only pretending when he tried laughing with them. After a while Mr Ghosh gave up trying to join in, but continued to be secretly jealous and watchful. More so because not only was Amolan young, handsome and a raconteur to boot, but he was also unemployed—his afternoons were free.

Mr Ghosh began to wish he had never won that second car in the Milky Munchy Mints contest. He didn't know where his wife drove herself in the afternoons. It was quite possible that she was going out with Amolan. It might have begun with an innocent shopping excursion. Then maybe a matinee. Possibly they had graduated to having lunch and coffee. And then... At this point in his imaginings, Mr Ghosh would irritably go and spend the rest of the evening in the company of his beetles. And because he tended to be a coward, he never said anything. A cold fear had begun joining palms with his heated jealousy. He began to be afraid that she might leave him. And because his cowardice made him vindictive, he would often take the keys of the second car with him when he drove to work. In the evening he would pretend he had forgotten that they were in his pocket. When Mrs Ghosh put on her best sari to go out with him, he would tell her the colour didn't suit her, and ask her to change so that she looked less attractive. At night he would give her painful love bites on her neck so that the next day she would have to leave her thick, black hair flowing down her back in order to hide the purple patches on her delicate skin. She couldn't go out like that, and if Amolan visited her, thought Mr Ghosh grimly, he would see proof of Mr Ghosh's ownership. When Mrs Ghosh bent over his desk with his evening tea tray, he would often squeeze her breast brutally; he was quite sure it hurt. She never said anything. But her large, dark eyes would look puzzled, and a thin crease would appear between the graceful sweep of her eyebrows. It was frustrating. Mr Ghosh wished she would say something, protest, so that he could tell her angrily that she was his, that her body was his. But she never did. And, glowering angrily, he would spend evening after evening at his desk, his shiny bald patch bent over his shiny, spread-eagled beetles. At such times he wished that Mrs Ghosh would shrink so that he could keep her in a jar. Like a little live beetle. After dinner, when they sat in their comfortable drawing room, their conversation was of the most mundane variety and even that began to dwindle away. While Mr Ghosh scoured various newspapers for contest opportunities, she would look silently through baby patterns in crochet magazines. Pretending, thought Mr Ghosh maliciously, that she was going to have a baby.

It was during one of those unbearable, interminable post-dinner silences that it first occurred to Mr Ghosh that he should try using his willpower to win another kind of contest. It was as if a little red switch in his brain had been casually but deftly flicked into the 'on' position. If he won, it would be the victory of his life. There could be no real contest between the thin, angular and balding Mr Ghosh, and the handsome, youthful Amolan. This much Mr Ghosh grudgingly conceded. But he would win the contest as he had won every other. And in the same fell blow he would show Mrs Ghosh to whom she belonged. When the thought first slipped into his mind, it was as a kind of bitter fantasy. Looking over the top of his newspaper at his wife, he imagined a tiny version of her sitting in the palm of his hand, like a mermaid stranded in a landlocked desert. It gave him a strange pleasure to imagine her thus, and the thought almost never failed to bring a slight curl to his lip. When it first took shape as a serious idea, he was appalled. Not so much by the ludicrousness of it all, as by the possibility that he was going insane. It was fantastically horrible that such a thought should occur to him and stay with him. But stay it did, like a not entirely unwelcome guest. Like a predatory beetle it wormed its way into his very core.

One evening, after dinner, he decided he would do it. He would use the full might of his willpower to shrink his wife. She would be his in every way. In a glass jar, with air holes in the lid. Like a little live beetle. When she had learned her lesson he would will her back to her original size. Or then again, he might not. A little lump of pungent phlegm slid down Mr Ghosh's throat. By now, he had reached a point in his jealous musings when it seemed more than likely to him that his fiendish, fantastic, impossible plan would work. There was no reason why it shouldn't, he thought, when his willpower had helped him win every other contest. It was just that this contest was a little different. And the manner of winning, a little unusual. He thought it ironic and unfair to have to try and win back what was rightfully his in the first place, but he really had no choice. It never occurred to him just how ghastly it would be for Mrs Ghosh if she were shrunk and made to live in a glass jar. It never occurred to him that anyone might quite conceivably die of shock if such a thing ever happened to them.

So it was that he stopped looking through newspapers for new contests. He wanted to concentrate all his energies on winning this Contest of Contests. He was so absorbed in this task that he found it difficult to concentrate at work. Instead, he constantly focused on mentally dissecting Mrs Ghosh and then willing her individual limbs, head, fingers, torso, to shrink. This went on for several weeks. Every morning he would wake up and look at his wife to see if she had begun shrinking. But Mrs Ghosh would be lying there in her pink nightdress, fast asleep, as innocent as an angel. And definitely, most positively, the same size as she had been the day before.

As each morning commenced thus, Mr Ghosh was consumed by frustration and despair. Each day his jealousy intensified. He started making surprise telephone calls to his house. When the reply was only a monotonous ringing, he would concentrate on the shrinking process with the fury and vigour of a madman. If Mrs Ghosh picked up the phone, he would make up some unimportant question to ask her. At other times he would simply disconnect the line quietly. Then the thought struck him that even if she was at home, it was entirely possible that Amolan was with her. He would imagine Mrs Ghosh putting the phone receiver down while Amolan caressed her bare waist. And yet, how composed, how slyly composed, she looked when her husband returned home in the evening!

Soon Mr Ghosh could bear it no longer. The more he willed his wife to shrink, the more tortured his thoughts became. In his study, enclosed by the red, monolithic curtains, his evenings with his rows of beetles grew longer. He went to bed later and later. He woke in the mornings earlier and earlier. He was losing vast amounts of sleep and energy due to his extraordinary feat of continuous concentration. And he ate with a vigorous appetite to replenish that energy. Soon Mrs Ghosh had to buy more rice, fish, meat and vegetables during her weekly shopping. The more she cooked, the more her husband ate. She was an excellent cook and had no trouble serving up large quantities of Mr Ghosh's favourite dishes. Potato curry. Fish curry. Biryanis of all kinds. Parathas stuffed with spicy minced meats or crumbly paneer delights. Hot samosas. Syrupy jalebis. He started carrying an abundance of food in his office tiffin. When everyone else was busy working at their desks, he snacked on high energy candy bars, surreptitiously and with enjoyment. Consequently, his chin grew thick. His shoulders forged an alliance with his head so that his neck all but disappeared. His waistline surged forward to meet his arms. His bony fingers acquired a bulbous globule of fat at each tip. His teeth grew yellow because of his habit of nibbling chocolate in bed, too lazy to get up and brush his teeth before falling asleep. In the span of a few months, Mr Ghosh flabbergasted everyone around him by going from thin and lanky to fat and round. Only his head retained its small, bony shape so that it looked like a brown cherry perched on top of a giant chocolate fudge sundae. Compared to the rest of him, his arms seemed undergrown and thin. And, like all fat people, he started to look short. Mr Ghosh had never been a particularly sprightly man, but now he was positively sluggish. His mind, however, had never been more active. Day after day his willpower was on overdrive, forced and pushed beyond belief in the single-minded pursuit of his goal. He was driven relentlessly by the prospect of holding a little live beetle of unique provenance in the palm of his hand. And all the time, while he thought, willed and concentrated, he ate.

One morning, several months after Mr Ghosh had hatched his fiendish plan to possess his wife forever, Mrs Ghosh woke up earlier than usual. She looked at the alarm clock on her bedside table and saw that it was only five o'clock. She was surprised. She liked to sleep late in the mornings and never woke before seven, when it was time to prepare Mr Ghosh's breakfast. After he had left for the office, she would have another snooze till about nine-thirty, read the papers till ten, and then go into the bathroom for a hot, luxurious shower which lasted well over twenty minutes. This being Mrs Ghosh's morning routine, she was rather annoyed at feeling so wide awake at this odd, early hour. She licked the stale sleep off her beautiful, pouting lips and lay on her back, trying to relax her body so that she could fall asleep again. But she couldn't sleep and she couldn't relax. There was a funny feeling inside her. Not quite nausea. But definitely an uneasy sensation. As if something was going to happen. A few minutes later, feeling distinctly uncomfortable, she turned to wake Mr Ghosh. He wasn't there. His green pyjamas were there, laid out neatly like a deflated green balloon. Mrs Ghosh sat up in bed in wonder, and then gave a little scream. A small brown beetle was lying on Mr Ghosh's pillow, spread-eagled on its back with its tiny legs kicking furiously in the air.

It was all over very quickly after that: she reached for the can of pesticide she always kept under her bed, and sprayed for all she was worth. At first the legs kicked even more frantically, but after a while they slowed down, as if they were tired. Finally, they became quite still and a silence filled the room. That was when Mrs Ghosh, handkerchief to her nose, realized that a small hum that had filled the air while the beetle was alive had stopped. She looked closely at the little creature and her expression changed.

Slowly, Mrs Ghosh got out of bed. In silence she picked up yesterday's newspaper from the floor and walked across to the other side of the bed. Gently, but with a shaking hand, she scooped him up like a dead fly and stood looking down at the pudgy, naked body with the neck that had thickened into an extension of the shoulders. Fattened on her delicious curries and biryanis. The four angular limbs. Capped by the bulbous little cherry of a head.

After a while Mrs Ghosh slipped into her warm bedroom slippers and padded down the stairs. She opened the door to the still, red study and brought out the beetle-lined trays. Methodically, she arranged them all on the desk and then stepped back thoughtfully, as if she were choosing a shade of lipstick. Then she brought out a thin silver pin from a drawer and carefully added one more item to Mr Ghosh's prized collection.

'This is the best place for you,' she whispered. The rising sun threw a splash of honey across the room and her beautiful lips parted to reveal a sparkling smile.

Thank God for Star Trek

Bombay is a cone-shaped city. It is a gulping creature. Processions of things and beings tumble in at the wide end, and out the narrow end emerges a mulch of heat, perspiration, headaches, nausea, indigestion, depression, and time standing still on a hot afternoon because the noon sun will not budge or blink its blazing eye. It burns the eyes of schoolchildren as they head home, and singes them at lunch break when escape from the high-ceilinged, wooden-desked classrooms is countered by the sun glinting down meanly; and the children's eyes, aching from lack of sleep and no lack of squinting at textbooks, turn inwards and create heat headaches that are actually book headaches and teacher headaches and home headaches and the itchy headaches of sweat pooling in the corners of the eye and the hot hidden space behind the ear. In a daze of heat, chewing bubblegum to distract themselves from the gnawing headaches and lack of rest, teeth wedged with specks of masala chips, the children go home, hunchbacked carriers of school bags.

When Sunday finally arrives, eleven-year-old Anshu is lying on her back, blearily staring at the cracked plaster on the ceiling. This morning she feels a headache coming on. She turns away from the ceiling as consciousness of the day comes over her. It is late and bright outside. She cannot remember why she has a heavy feeling in her throat. The sunshine that falls into the room in a solid, slanting column nauseates her with its glare. She staggers to the bathroom, loosening her pyjama cord. She brushes her teeth and re-emerges into the bedroom to the smell of freshly buttered toast. Hard biscuit-like pieces of toast lie on a plate, with a mug of hot milk and a glass of water next to it. Another Sunday, the dreaded day of homework and horrible anticipation of Monday. A day of sloth and slightly throbbing headaches in her temples, caused by a late morning, unevenly spaced meals and snacks, and the indigestion that inevitably comes with it. Mamma is speaking on the phone. She gestures towards the breakfast and Anshu obediently begins eating. The toast is delicious, buttery and salty. But she lets the milk stand, she hates it. She hates it even more five minutes later because a slimy, creamy skin has formed on its surface. Mamma puts the phone down and comes towards Anshu, smiling. She is wearing a lemon-yellow sari of soft cotton, decorated with yellow and green buds.

'Good morning, darling,' she says softly, hugging her daughter. Anshu looks at her mother's lovely face, her breath fresh with toothpaste, her cotton sari soft and smelling of detergent, her neck warm and inviting.

The heaviness inside her has not dissipated. She buries her head in her mother's neck and puts her arms around her shoulders. Two small tears trickle down her cheeks.

Mamma lifts Anshu's chin and looks into her face, puzzled and concerned. But her eyes appear preoccupied. 'What's the matter?'

'I don't know,' says Anshu, her voice muffled in the folds of the sari on her mother's neck.

'Then stop crying, my baby,' is the soft answer. 'Come, have your breakfast. Have your milk.'

Anshu then has to drink the lukewarm milk after scooping off some of the slimy layer. She cannot control herself anymore and the tears gush forth.

'What's the matter, do you have too much homework for tomorrow?'

Anshu is not sure whether that is the matter. The answer is no, but she says yes.

'What is the homework?'

'I have to colour all the states of India and label them correctly and also colour the sea around and I haven't even started. I have to colour them very lightly and evenly, and I can never get it right.'

Her mother says nothing for a moment. In another moment the pause tips over into a silence. Anshu glances at her with fear in her heart.

'Do it after lunch,' suggests her mother. 'Watch your TV shows first.'

So Anshu flops down in front of the television and watches *Star Trek,* an episode where Captain Kirk is fighting a giant lizard on a brown planet. She slips into the Sunday morning routine, which is like slithering down a sticky slide, letting the day drain away into the white glare of the afternoon and the heavy, humid sea breezes of the evening. During the advertisements, her mother goes out, saying she will be back at teatime. Anshu feels the usual panic in her stomach. Will she come back? What if something happens to her and I never see her again? The panic subsides as *Star Trek* comes on again. She feels fat and bloated as she continues to sit dozily and watch the screen, though her arms are long and delicate, and her shoulders border on the bony. She is not the full-cheeked, strong-boned, hearty type, has never been the kind of girl who screams with laughter playing catch-catch or running races. Of late she has turned into a sickly sort of child, continually falling ill with one minor affliction after another. A cold for a day, a stomach cramp for a few hours, a sore throat for a week. The doctor has instructed her to increase her food intake, but all this has done is develop an unpleasant layer of fat on her belly.

The morning drags on, and after the TV programmes, she drags herself into the shower. Afterwards she looks at her room in distaste. There is a small heap of story books on the floor. The previous day she had ambitiously decided to start a little library and begin numbering and labelling her books. But she only got as far as pulling all the books off their shelves. And now they lie there messy and unnumbered and the whole idea of a library seems boring and stupid. Between then and now, the pile has somehow got mixed up with her school books and the clothes she wore yesterday. She walks into the mess, picks out a book she wants to read, and flops down on the sofa with it.

After a while the cook calls out to her to come and have lunch. She eats silently with her nose buried in the book, not noticing the food, and consequently eats far more than she needs. She feels even more bloated and staggers back to her room, her head throbbing slightly, to colour the map. She cannot find the light blue pencil for the sea. When she finally locates it she sees that the point is broken. But the sharpener is lost so she has to use the dark blue pencil instead. She can remember someone getting a C for using the wrong colours. She uses a light, careful hand and thinks it might be an acceptable substitute for light blue. Quickly she begins colouring Himachal a nice bright red. With a thud in her chest she remembers too late—cool colours for the cool states, hot colours for the hot states. She starts colouring over the red with green—Himachal then appears as a kind of sunset melting onto a light-green lawn. She only has one copy of the map though, so all she can do is bite her lip and worry. It is five o'clock before the map is done. Why, oh why, does she never finish her homework earlier, why does it always have to trickle down to the last minute of the weekend, spoiling everything?

The sun is beginning its descent. The Archie comics from the local library look faded and sickening in the diminishing light. The hollow feeling in Anshu's stomach grows. She has spent the whole day alone, and now it overwhelms her. Her spirit recoils from the air that enwraps her, the space around her that has moved her of its own accord through the routine of this dull Sunday. She is condemned to stand by the open window, oppressed by the quickening stirrings of the sea air which make the back of her neck tingle and raise goosebumps at the bottom of her spine. The day is turning, the sun is setting, the blue-white of the sky is deepening fast, the kites, crows, pigeons, sparrows cry out as they head home and settle down to await the night, the honking of the evening traffic rises into the air as hundreds of cars wend their way home, the day is in flux and everything in motion. Only Anshu stands still at the window in the fading light, hating these changes, this motion around her of things, birds, people, settling into their rightful places, this motion that has left her out so completely, her heart beating with sadness and fear, waiting for her mother to return.

◡

She does return. But everything is different these days. Anshu thinks about 'these days', but in fact it has been so many days that she cannot remember exactly how and when everything changed so much. But nowadays, and for many, many days past, Mamma will not be still. She will not be peaceful and she will not be snug and warm. She gazes with a hard expression around the apartment, she moves about dusting things, she takes out old photo albums and then puts them away without opening them, starts writing letters but does not finish them, she will not settle down to any one thing. She opens all the windows wide, in every room, as if this is imperative to be able to breathe. The warm wind that runs lightly along the surface of the Arabian Sea enters the apartment and explores it in little gusts that butt their way around corners and flutter the pages of the book Anshu is reading; or it comes in swirls of cool draughts that run wild through the large apartment, making the heavy, floor-length curtains billow out and flap, emitting a hollow, drum-like sound. At such times Anshu feels as if the ground is slipping away under her feet, and she feels small and oppressed like an insect in a buzzing hive. What has come before and what will come after grow distant and confused in her mind, and all she can do is try to focus on the task at hand, continually interrupted by the sounds of her mother and the wind moving around their home. She then plunges into reading comic book after comic book, drugging herself with the inhabitants of a faraway place in America called Riverdale, where alien and exciting things like sundaes and hotdogs are an everyday affair, and where school is a den of friends and dates. But when she puts down the last comic book in the pile, exhausted and eyes aching, the heaviness in her chest is still there. As if she had never touched her comics.

⌣

The monsoon arrives with its usual ferocity. Rivers of rain cascade down for days and wrap the city in a muggy blanket. Every year Anshu marvels at the wet metallic rainbows left on the pitch-black roads. Each year she asks in wonder, 'How come there are rainbows on the road?' and her mother tells her why. But this year she doesn't ask, because for the first time she remembers it without any prompting. For the first time her mother does not say 'Vibgyor' in her clear high voice because Anshu has no need to ask her annual question, 'What's that word for the rainbow colours?' This time she recites the word and the colours to herself, not to her mother. And for the first time she feels sick at the sight of the spilled petrol rainbows because they make the road look slippery and slimy. The oily colours only seem to add to the noxious fumes that rise from the honking roads.

At home, ordinary conversation is replaced by the whistles of the wind that squeezes through the chinks in the wooden window frames even when they are shut tight. When the phone rings its clang shrieks like an echo in an empty house, though their home is full of things. She does not dare to ask her mother questions. It is easier, just easier, waiting for everything to get better again. Though she can remember less and less what better felt and looked like; slowly she has got used to the feeling of waiting, though she cannot clearly picture what she is waiting for.

One afternoon, after school, Anshu remembers that her mother will not be back for a few hours. What is the point of going home? She dreads another solitary afternoon in the vastness of her apartment. In the sandpit she climbs up the uneven bars and ladders of the jungle gym and sits perched up there as the school ground empties out and she tries to delay the inevitable. When the guard comes around banging his stick on the ground and looks at her with an enquiring frown, she clambers down, picks up her heavy school satchel and walks slowly to the bus stop. It is almost empty as the first crush of children and parents is gone. The next bus soon arrives, careening around the corner. Anshu does not get off at the stop near her home. She stays in the bus till it reaches the long, sweeping walkway along the Worli Sea Face. It is an extra half-hour on the bus, quite a long way from home, but she can't think of anywhere else to go. Mamma likes to come here sometimes to look at the sea and stroll down the walkway, with Anshu trailing her and contentedly digging her teeth into a roasted corncob rubbed with lemon juice and chilli powder. It seems natural and a very good idea to go for a stroll there herself.

She stands facing the sea uncertainly. The air is soft and feather-like, for there was a quick heavy shower about two hours earlier, pushing the glaring sun behind misty clouds and painting the sky a pleasant blue. The walkway along the sea face is almost empty. The few passers-by look at her oddly. Suddenly she becomes aware that she is doing something drastically different and daring. Exhilaration at escaping the silence and loneliness of home lasts a mere few moments before her mind shrinks back in fear. She has never been allowed to go out unaccompanied like this. How strange she must look, a child of eleven, all alone, standing with her school bag, looking at the sea. What if her mother returned home early? She would be sick with worry. Around these thoughts grows increasing dread, and after a few steps this way and that as if to walk down the sea face and drink in the cool breeze, she quickly turns away to trudge back to the bus stop. Her eyes fall on a lonely figure sitting on the parapet about twenty metres away, looking down at the waves that chop and churn against the black boulders beneath. She stops in her tracks, in a panic at being found out, but unable to take her gaze from the awful scene of her mother's desolation. At that moment, with terrifying accuracy, her mother turns her head and looks straight into Anshu's eyes. For a few seconds they stare at each other. Anshu's soles are rooted to the concrete. Even from that distance she feels her mother's glance curdling into a cold fury. Quaking and with tears in her throat, she turns and runs to the bus stop, her heavy satchel bumping hard into the small of her back. She doesn't know what she has done wrong, but it feels towering, mountainous, annihilating.

When she reaches home the cook has a message for her.

'You just missed your Mamma's phone call. She is going to be home late tonight, so you are not to wait for her for dinner. I'll get it ready early, might as well get it out of the way,' says the cook as she sits on her haunches shelling peas, her old face peering through the V shape made by her bony legs and knees.

Anshu listens in silence and then runs into the bathroom where she sobs as noiselessly as possible. Then, with wide dry eyes, she does her homework, has her dinner and gets into the big double bed about two hours earlier than usual. Her mother always sleeps holding Anshu in her arms as if she were a small child. But tonight she wants to avoid seeing her mother because she is terrified. She will be asleep when Mamma returns, and then in the morning everything will be all right. But she cannot sleep. She builds a cave for herself under the blanket and looks at the pinpricks of dim light that show through and pretends they are stars. She will remain in her cave, she says to herself, and in fact she will fall asleep here, self-sufficient and in a kind of a dark Stone Age world of her own making. But a few minutes later, she kicks off the blanket because it is too hot.

Two hours later, Anshu is still awake—she hears her mother enter the apartment, go into the bathroom, turn on the tap, brush her teeth. She hears all the dull thuds and bumps that accompany a person moving about in a quiet house, but she keeps her face turned to the wall and her eyes squeezed shut. The noises stop. She has a strong feeling that her mother is standing over her, looking down at her. She is sure she feels a presence at her bedside, a shift in the coordinates of things on her side of the bed. She listens carefully for the sound of breathing but hears nothing. Could it be that Mamma is holding her breath so that Anshu will not know she is there? There she stands, looking down at her daughter. A hot pounding begins in Anshu's ears, so loud that it must be obvious that she is awake. Then she will get into trouble for pretending to be asleep. She will look very carefully. So she opens her eyes a slit. There is no one there. She opens her eyes fully and looks at the empty space. There is no Mamma. Then she turns and sees a dark shape lying still next to her. Relief is followed by wretchedness, and the bed is no more a sanctuary. Mamma didn't even say goodnight.

That night Anshu has a nightmare in which the city is a maze made up of a confusing grid of skyscrapers and ever-moving cars. The air is humid and poisonous, a mix of sea-water droplets and petrol fumes that rise unending from the vehicles. Streets run between the cars like tunnels and warrens. Skyscrapers tower above the pulsating grid, the spaces between them creating vertical windy hollows stretching up and up. Her mother wanders the grid, wearing her lemon-yellow sari, her hair tied neatly in a bun, looking for something, looking for a way out. Anshu can see the way out, and runs in to tell her mother, look, here is the way, this way, come out this way. It is confusing navigating the maze, for it shifts as the cars move this way and that, orderly but relentless in their movements, obeying some unfathomable law of infinite motion. Anshu keeps feeling that she is approaching her mother, but then loses sight of her for a second as she turns a corner, only to find, when she comes into view again, that she is now even further away. She does not turn and look at Anshu, but keeps walking, searching. And then Anshu's guts turn cold as she sees her mother looking back at her with a smile and then walking on and she realizes that her mother is not looking for a way out but for a way further in, into the entrails of the maze. She wakes with a scream in her throat and her scalp wet with perspiration. It is quiet. The ceiling fan mutely beats at the air.

In the morning her mother stares at Anshu in silence as she gulps down her milk and toast. Then her voice cuts through the stillness and Anshu looks up in despair.

'Anshu,' she says, in a hard, biting voice, 'don't ever spy on me again.'

Anshu has a miserable day at school. She has forgotten to learn her twelve times tables. She hopes desperately that the teacher won't pick her to say them. One after another girls stand up and say them, some halting, some fluent, but everyone has learned them. The teacher looks at her contemptuously but leaves her alone. In English class, the teacher gives them an exercise where they have to write in two columns, as fast as they can, the names of things that are hard and things that are soft. In the 'hard' column, she writes: biscuits, toast, eyes, teeth, sand, pencil point, sun, points of light. In the 'soft' column she writes: sari, lemons, hair, shampoo, neck, blanket, fur, kitten. The teacher says that eyes, sand and the sun are not hard. Lemons are not soft. Pencil point and points of light are marked as 'Repetition'. The teacher called it a baby exercise, but her page has thick red crosses and the word 'Poor' scratched on it. She looks around the room. The other girls wear relaxed expressions and slouch easily in their chairs, twiddling their pencils.

When she returns home in the afternoon, sticky with sweat,

she looks uncertainly into the bedroom. Her mother is reading a magazine and smiles at her. Anshu smiles back.

Only two more days till *Star Trek* comes on again.

The Mall

I have been wandering in this shopping mall for about a year. My hair is stringy and my armpits are hairy, and in my many shopping bags are things I bought a long time ago with my credit card.

There are others like me. I see them now and then. There is a short, squat woman in a voluminous sari that makes her look like a puff pastry. I have seen her exchanging hellos with a bored middle-aged couple. This couple trudges about the mall with glazed eyes and dragging feet, looking into every shop window they pass. Their cheeks sag with fat. They have both put on weight in the past year, and they both walk in the same way, an indolent, hip-swaying progression, she in her grey, cotton salwar-kameez, he in his brown-patterned shirt. They haven't noticed me yet, but the short, squat woman has. She's sharp, that one, which leads me to mull over why she hasn't yet found a way to leave. We could pool our resources, stick together like a tribe and muscle our way out somehow, but we're too different. I wouldn't know what to say to any of them, though the short, squat woman has, in the past, given me a slight weary smile when we passed each other. That was in the days following my sole attempt at communication with her. Then there are the two young girls, perhaps twenty years old, wearing skinny jeans. They are thin like chopsticks, with uneven skin as if recently recovered from a bout of chocolate acne. They carry small silly purses that look flat and empty and cheap, and they laugh. How they giggle, their heads and shoulders leaning into each other, exchanging interminable confidences, and they walk incessantly, the awkward walk of a blind insect that has no idea where it and its many legs are going. How they still have any confidences to exchange after a year of being stuck at the hip eludes me. They irritate me, these two. And yet I'm fascinated by them, because I have a suspicion that grows stronger by the day—they have no idea how long they have been here or that they are trapped, so absorbed are they with each other and their meandering walkabout.

My terrible ordeal began last May. Everyone was talking about the new mall. As I walked in, its frosty blast of air instantly evaporated the summer heat on my skin. There was a central atrium which shot up skywards to what seemed to be the tenth or fifteenth floor. This column, topped with a glass dome, was simply the spinal column, so to say, of a gargantuan creature. There were escalators everywhere. Most notably, one that went straight to the fourth floor in a sweeping circular motion like a wide spiral staircase. From the sixth floor it was possible to take an escalator directly down to the third. A couple of other escalators performed similar acrobatics, flamboyant distractions from the ordinary ones. The mall was an architectural feat. Its owners clearly had grand ambitions, for their motto, emblazoned everywhere, was: 'This is not a mall.' This teaser was then paired with various explanatory phrases. I read on a banner: 'This is not a mall. It is the better side of life.' Elsewhere I read: 'This is not a mall. It is a garden of possibilities.' There were others I came across in the course of the year. Needless to say, later, when I realized that I could not leave, these words seemed menacing. I spent long hours pondering their meaning. More and more, the assertion that this was not a mall seemed to me not a motto but a disclaimer.

But in the beginning I was thrilled with this palace of pleasure. Here was the promise of many happy shopping hours.

On that first day, I was on the sixth floor, wandering down the curved path circling the atrium. On my right were wide walkways lined with shops, radiating out from the central shaft. On my left was the plunge down to the atrium, like a deep, brightly lit well. Jutting out from the sides of this well were gay little mezzanine floors, holding the chairs and tables of various cafés and restaurants. It looked like a giant puzzle; it felt as if you could reach down and slide any of these floors back into the walls, snap them into place without seam or fuss. And if you looked up, there was the domed skylight, and you felt you were floating in a wide column that opened to the sky, all brilliant blue and wispy clouds.

Just below me, on one of the mezzanine floors that partially obstructed this slightly terrifying drop, I spotted Radha. She was sitting at a table with a plate of salad and three large shopping bags, one of which, I noticed, was Louis Vuitton. Radha, Radha, I called, but she didn't hear me. I wanted to know what she'd bought but she was talking into her cell phone. I texted her and moved on.

I stopped at Veronika, a cool new Russian boutique selling cosmetics. I found a gorgeous brown eyeshadow, a set of three earth-toned lipsticks, and essence of orange blossom. Everything came individually wrapped in tissue, in an enormous floral paper bag.

Then I dived into Malleys, a department store so big it had four sets of its own escalators.

Now what happened next was a very specific train of events. One thing led to another, as it were. In Malleys I hoped my lucky run with cosmetics would continue, but I found myself doing a bored glide through a maze of Estée Lauder and Clinique and Issey Miyake and-so-on counters. It was all a bit too common, and besides, I thought, I have all these brands, why don't they come up with something new and exclusive, how can they expect us to go on buying the same old things over and over again?

Then, in a quiet corner, I heard a pleasant gurgling, like a clear brook running over pigeon-grey pebbles. On beautiful display was a new brand of perfume called…Pigeon Grey! The packaging was elegant, aristocratic.

Did the countesses and duchesses of Old England have carrier pigeons, was this line inspired by that aristocratic life? I asked the girl behind the counter. She was, of course, a dumb nitwit wearing the orange and yellow colours of the mall. I only wanted to see whether she even knew what a carrier pigeon was.

Ma'am? She opened her eyes wide and gazed at the tester bottle in her hand. Then she went into default mode, arm extended to emit a spray.

I ignored her and examined the display. The box was a delicate grey tinged with powder blue, and its logo was a single small pigeon embossed in black detail. It was the sort of thing to splash on for sunset cocktails, where you want to be outstandingly dressed but in an understated way—the sort of tricky occasion where it's twilight when you arrive, so you can't be in all-out glamorous evening wear, and dark when you leave so you can't be in daylight colours either. That is the kind of perfume this is, I thought. It felt reassuring to know there was a company out there that understood such subtleties.

Do you have any other Pigeon Grey products? I asked. Ma'am, the other products in the range will only arrive in December. For God's sake, you people... I'll have to pick some up when I go to London one of these days, I said, wrinkling my nose. She simply stared at me. I took the tester and spritzed it on my wrist. I was sold, it was magic!

I blinked at the price, which hasn't happened in a while. But I bought it, of course.

I was done with cosmetics.

There were four more women's floors in Malleys, one each for designer wear, casuals, lingerie and shoes. Nice, very nice, I thought, a real range of choice. I started on the designer floor, and headed for Alberta Ferretti. I picked out a shrug, a belt, a pencil skirt and a bustier, and tried them on. Everything looked pretty good except for the bustier which looked tarty even with the shrug. I took it all off and went looking for another top.

Then I saw it: an off-shoulder pea-green dress. All thoughts of the pencil skirt ensemble went out the window.

In my pea-green dress I felt myself blush and come alive. There are few things in the world as moving as the discovery of an outfit that wraps you in a soft, full-body embrace. It kissed my skin. It cupped my breasts. It loved me. And the mirror said wow.

In celebration, I kept the pencil skirt ensemble too.

On I went, through Ferragamo, Cavalli, Prada. I picked up a silk scarf, a leather wallet, a tennis frock, a brunch jacket. But my heart wasn't in it. I wanted shoes for my pea-green dress. I wanted to make it perfect.

So I rode up two floors on the escalator to the shoe section, shopping bags dangling wrist to elbow. I saw pumps, soft, emerald, Italian leather. I rubbed the hide between my fingers, lingering for a few moments, and then proceeded to find colours in sea greens and mushroom, which would all do, but I didn't want to make do. Neither Jimmy Choo nor DKNY made the cut. I hunted all over the shoe floor, it was the biggest I had ever seen. It was a sea of shoes. And then, in a far corner I spotted land. It appeared to be a new designer brand. It was called Two Peas in a Pod. I headed over and couldn't believe my eyes. Two Peas in a Pod made shoes and bags exclusively in shades of pea-green! So much variety in one colour was overwhelming. There were about forty designs just in platform pumps. I tried on dozens of pairs, pencil point stilettos, strappy sandals, chunky heels, peep-toes, pointy toes—an indefatigable assistant kept bringing me more and more. Eventually I was so confused that I felt I must put on the dress and then try on the shoes.

But this floor sold only shoes and bags, so there were no changing rooms. The assistant told me that I need not go down two floors again. There was a changing room just one floor below. Down the escalator I went. But this was the goat-class floor with the mass label clothes. It was teeming with women, not like the quiet designer floor downstairs. After waiting in line for a while at the changing rooms, I went back to the escalators. Down at the designer floor I found an empty changing room at once, and, feeling like a bungler for wasting time, I put on the pea-green dress. Looking unsuitably glamorous and showing an absurd amount of cleavage, I headed back up two floors on the escalator.

Back on the shoe floor, I found I had used the wrong escalator. I found myself in the unbranded shoe section, milling with people. There appeared to be a sale going on. I had to crane my neck over people's heads to see where Two Peas in a Pod was. But I figured it would be easier to simply walk across this floor, rather than go down again and find the correct escalator up.

It was a tiresome business. I shuffled along through the crowd and the racks of bags and shoes. Cheap leather and resin piled high here, stuffed into racks there, so much of it that the odour sickened me, no doubt the effect of being combined with acres of human skin. I began to feel disgusted at the rubbing and the touching. My skin, exposed to a large extent because of the pea-green dress with its low back and short length, kept coming into contact with other people's skin. The cheap-shoe crowd was never-ending and the shoe hall was vast.

And the noise! Like a halo of tweeting Disney birds circling my head. Scraps of music floated litter-like above the clamour. For a breather, I took a smart side-step into a relatively quiet aisle. No wonder it was quiet because the stuff here was ghastly. Rows of bags and shoes made of red resin, covered in shiny shit-brown splotches, displayed on five-foot-high racks. I looked at the three or four people here. Among them was the bored, overweight couple, whom I recognized later as among the trapped. I gave up the riddle of what they found so gripping in this aisle and plunged back into the crowd of shuffling women.

But I had lost my bearings. Far to my left I saw some embroidered clutch purses; I thought I had seen them before, so I turned to the right and once again began the interminable shuffling along. People are so sluggish, I thought in disgust. On the way I looked desultorily at the things on display. I was fed up to the bone, but I looked out of habit. To my annoyance my arm reached out to pick up a black handbag. Pea-green shoes, I reminded myself, but I was rather taken by this bag.

I slid into the side aisle. Many of the handbags here were surprisingly well-designed. Cheap as dirt, I thought, but looks like a million bucks, why not buy it. A salesgirl materialized. Yes, ma'am, she smiled, this way to the cashier please. Thank the lord, a sense of direction. I followed her obediently to pay at a till, and asked her how to get to Two Peas in a Pod. She looked befuddled. If I ever become a murderess, I thought, the victim will be a moronic salesgirl. Method of assassination: squeezing hard on the neck. Vaguely she said, ma'am, please go back down the aisle where you picked up this purse. But isn't there another route, I said, impatiently, it's very crowded there. She shook her head and said, ma'am, it's crowded on this side too.

Too true. Back I went down the black purse aisle and emerged where I had started. Except that I was now carrying one more shopping bag. I felt immensely irritated at myself for wasting time. I must have been half an hour buying the purse. I rustled among my shopping bags and took it out. It was so ordinary that I almost gagged at having squandered my time on it instead of going straight to Two Peas in a Pod.

Shuffle, shuffle, shuffling along. I felt like one card in a deck being shuffled slowly through a vast shuffling machine. At least I would be among the picture cards, I thought; more specifically, one of the queens, and not a faceless number card like the two of clubs that had been shuffling by my side for God knows how long. I don't think she knew where she was going or what she wanted to buy even. I looked down in disdain at the top of her head, flecked with oily dandruff, and then craned my neck again in despair.

Twice on the way I stepped into side aisles, once to pick up a leather belt and the second time to look at some travel pouches which looked interesting from a distance but tacky from up close. That cost me time and metres. I was now carrying seven or eight large shopping bags and my arms were beginning to tire.

I felt my phone vibrating in my purse. It was Radha.

Hi, babe, where are you, want to join me for coffee? I'd love to, I said, suddenly feeling exhausted and miserable, but I'm stuck on the stupid bag and shoe floor of Malleys, and I just can't find what I'm looking for. We decided I would meet her on mezzanine floor 7A at the café a bit later. Cool, she said, hanging up. And as she said 'cool', I felt a cool breeze hit me, for there was an inconspicuous exit beside a pillar that said 'Designer labels'. I made a crazy diagonal lunge for it—how the people obstructed my way with their sluggishness!—and once again I was back in a sparsely populated domain of hushed voices. A short distance behind me, almost hidden by artful pillars and mirrors, I could see the crowds I had escaped.

Now I could get the pea-green shoes. But first I wanted to spoil myself. I felt petulant and peevish at being squashed among those downmarket shoppers. It was supremely pleasurable to browse here, knowing I could afford almost anything. I felt like the queen of hearts, and coincidentally I happened upon a spectacular handbag by Niccolo Lamy, appliquéd with a design in hearts. I bought it.

I saw a sign, then, that said 'Way to Elevators', and next to it 'Thank you for visiting Malleys'. All at once I felt suffocated in Malleys because I seemed to have spent hours here. I had been hearing the same piped music ever since the pencil skirt ensemble, and the smell of leather pervading this floor overwhelmed me with a sudden nausea. I would come back for the pea-green shoes later. I strode towards the exit, albeit with the disconcerting knowledge that I had spent an age doing everything except what I really needed to. But it was too exhausting to think about that now and I found myself standing at the edge of the atrium well again, free of the maze that was Malleys.

Meanwhile, the entire mall had become busier. Hundreds of people strolled along the path circling the well of the atrium.

I had to constantly dodge people gazing at shop windows, children intent on their ice-cream cones, mothers fussing over prams, none of these individuals looking to see where they were going. I sighed several times but there is nothing one can do in such a situation. People are annoying. I changed out of the pea-green dress in a restroom. I stepped onto a steep, double-storey escalator which provided a welcome sense of movement and space as I travelled up and up through the atrium well, altogether bypassing the electronics floor—I could see it as we glided by, all black dials and knobs—and arrived at a miscellaneous boutique floor. Small classy shops, manageable, no mazes to navigate. This was looking like happy valley again. I ended up with an exquisite crystal sugar bowl by R'Pra, a Swarovski Ganesh the size of a strawberry, and a set of fun table napkins by Tres Jolie Miss Molly, a small Canadian boutique which was a riot of colours, swirls of purple and crimson everywhere. How I enjoyed my many large shopping bags, all stiff art paper and soft fabric cords.

Now I could meet Radha.

I phoned her. Radha was still on mezzanine 7A. Hi Radha, I said brightly, I'm ready for that coffee if you are. Sure, babes, come on down. She said I should look for the green zone elevators that stopped at the mezzanine floors. I walked all around the well but saw only red zone elevators. These stopped at the non-mezzanine floors.

Since I was on floor 12, it seemed best to take a red zone elevator to floor 7, and then find my way to 7A from there.

Floor 7 was the kids' zone. I walked through thuggish robots and violet-haired dolls. I asked a salesgirl for the way to mezzanine 7A. It is accessed only by the green zone elevators, she said. But where are they, I said impatiently. Please go down to the atrium, ma'am, she said. But why isn't 7A accessible from 7, I demanded,

I can see it down there if I lean over, it's twenty metres below us.

She walked over to the railing and peered down into the well. 7A jutted out as an unevenly shaped platform. She was being obliging but I felt even more snappish. Haven't you seen it before, I said sharply, you work here every day. She appeared not to hear me above the blare of the electronic games nearby, but gazed down at 7A and turned to me with a bland smile. Yes, ma'am, it is right here. But you need to access the green zone elevators from the atrium, or else go to the skylight bar on the top floor. So the green zone elevators are accessible only from the bottom floor and the top floor? I asked, a little mollified by the geography of the mall forming in my head. No, ma'am, she said, you can also go down the Main Street Walkway on level 2, or— Never mind, I said, cutting her off, I'll go down to the atrium. It took me another ten minutes to find my way back to the elevators. The next one that arrived was going up, not down. So I decided to go up to the skylight bar and take the green zone elevators from there.

The skylight bar was all dim shadows and low blue lighting. Moody lounge music and waiters in black bow ties made me feel I had leapfrogged into 10 p.m. It irritated me. I was in no mood for this. Dark silhouettes of couples and small groups sat around tables sipping from straws and wide-rimmed cocktail glasses. The back of my neck was damp with sweat, my shoulders ached and my shopping bags knocked against my knees at every step. I was now walking around the top rim of the giant spinal column of the mall, all of which was the skylight bar. I plodded through the dense carpeting which pulled at my ankles in the most tiresome way, as if it wanted to absorb my feet. It slowed me down considerably. Where were the green zone elevators?

Glancing up at the skylight's glass dome, it suddenly dawned on me that it was only a ceiling lit up to look like clouds in a blue sky. I looked at my watch and saw with a start that it was 8 p.m. Of course, the sky wouldn't be blue.

At this point, my chest began to feel like a bloated Tetra Pak. I needed a break. Some fresh air. At least a window, just to look outside. I didn't want to meet Radha anymore. I simply ought to buy my pea-green shoes and get out. I walked back to the red zone elevator I had come up in, and rode down.

I had made a note of the correct entrance to Malleys on floor 5. It was the one sandwiched between a 1950s American Diner and one selling Bosch coffee machines. I found it easily.

Once more I was standing among the Niccolo Lamy collection that led to Jimmy Choo that led to Dale Farrington that led, hopefully, to Two Peas in a Pod. But then it all felt so dull, so unventilated. I felt so weary. I had fingered the bags and shoes here a dozen times, for a dozen hours. It was like a bad dream, going round in circles only to arrive back at the same place. I felt I was re-breathing my own stale breath.

I am not going to dive in here again, I thought in revulsion.

Once again I changed my plans. I would go to the atrium. And get out.

Back I went to the elevators, a strange panicked tingling in my hands. I took quick steps now, my shopping bags knocking my thighs, my calves hurting, feeling trapped by my own stupid indecision, vexed at wasting time.

I descended into the atrium, which I had previously simply hurried through. It was a cavernous circular hall, a kind of leaping off point, the gut of the behemoth, surrounded by exits and entrances to various departments and stores. Giant slabs of black and white marble made a vast geometrical pattern on the floor. Above rose the entire column of the mall, like a hollowed out high-rise building blaring bright. Families milled around, extracted money from ATMs, stopped at the popcorn and ice-cream stalls, or simply gazed up in bewildered admiration. It was like standing at a sort of base camp. I walked all around the atrium but there was no sign of an exit. I stepped into the entrance of Malleys and made for the first counter with a salesgirl. Where is the exit, I asked. Behind you, ma'am. No, no, I don't mean the exit of Malleys. I mean the exit of the mall. Ma'am, it's on level 3. But I entered at the atrium, I protested. No, ma'am, this is the basement. You entered on level 3.

I did not argue because I could not bear to look at her vapid face for another second. Perhaps she was right, perhaps not. I walked out slowly. I bought a Diet Coke from the popcorn stall and sat down at a small cluster of thin round tables. As I sipped wearily, the torsos of people brushed by me. There is a whole atrium out there, I thought in irritation, and yet people manage to brush past me like a cloud of flies.

Perhaps it was over-the-top on my part, but I was beginning to feel a little tearful. I was so very tired. I would hook up with Radha and leave with her. I dialled Radha.

Babes, where have you been, she said, we've all finished our coffees and shopping, we're on our way out. We? Who's we? I asked. I thought you were alone. No, no, we're all here, Betty, Mink, Vani, we're all done now. Wait, I said, I'll leave with you. We're already in the car, babes, catch you later. Wait, I said, what exit did you leave from? Why, she said. I'm kind of lost in this stupid place, I can't find the way out. There was a silence and then uncontrolled giggling, apparently from the entire car. Babes, look for signs that say Exit, she said, in a slow drawl. More laughter in the background. They were high on shopping and caffeine. I felt jealous at the thought of all of them in the car, going off home in high spirits. Why hadn't Radha told me they were all there together, I thought resentfully. I can't find the damned exit, yaar, I said, putting on a brave voice, a nonchalant one. What did you buy, she said. For a moment I couldn't remember, so irrelevant was the question to my present concerns. But I looked down at my tangle of bags and said, a crystal sugar bowl, a Niccolo Lamy bag, a Swarovski Ganesh... Oh you and your Swarovskis, she said, cutting me off. Her laugh was unkind. I did not want directions to the exit from her any more. Bye then, I said. Ciao, ciao, babes. The line went blank.

I hauled myself up and wound my way to the third floor, as directed by the Malley's salesgirl. I must have spent hours looking for the exit, wandering the sprawling walkways that radiated out from the central shaft, peering into the well for clues and signs, consulting the floor maps a dozen times, following the directions to the exits, unable to find a single one. I looked for a central information desk. There wasn't one.

I lost my phone. I plugged it into a public charging dock, turned my back for a minute, and it disappeared. All my numbers gone. Just like that. Such a head-spinning nausea gripped me then, I felt my guts would heave out. I swallowed the saliva and the panic gathering in my mouth, once, twice, ten times, forcing it down my throat. I made my way to the electronics floor to buy a new phone, only to discover they didn't sell SIM cards. I persuaded one of the orange-and-yellow-clad salesgirls to come with me to the map and explain the way out. I went up a floor, down a floor, asking other customers for directions. Are you about to leave, I began asking people, hoping that I could follow them out. Most looked puzzled and simply said no, we are not.

Finally, a middle-aged couple said yes, we are about to leave, and so I attached myself to them. We just need to buy a few things first, said the man, kindly. Their shopping went on for over an hour, during which time they kept turning to look at me in bemusement, but I gritted my teeth and stuck to my guns. I refused to walk away and waste the time I had already invested in them. Soon it became intolerable for both parties. The woman, in a floral salwar-kameez and a giant pink flower stuck into a black-dyed bun, leaned towards her husband and said something, glancing at me in distrust. The husband looked embarrassed, but turned to me and said, excuse me, madam, but why are you following us? You said you were about to leave, I spluttered in indignation, my voice heavy with tears. I need to get out! You can find the exit yourself, no, said the woman in a rather aggressive voice. Her husband began nodding and smiling at me, but pushed at her elbow to go. I backed off. I dragged yet another salesgirl out of her shop and demanded that she show me the way herself. When she said she was unable to leave her department, I lost my temper. What the hell do you people want, I hissed, money? You want money? I'll give you money. See, see here, see my shopping, all designer labels that show you I have money, money, money, I'll give you lots if you just take me to the damned exit. I lost my head, spewing out poisonous words at her. She kept trying to interrupt me, saying ma'am, ma'am, whenever I stopped for breath. Finally when I ran out of steam, I simply panted and glared at her. Ma'am, she said, please take the red zone elevator to level 5 and follow the exit signs through Malleys.

Late that night I held another can of Diet Coke in my hand, seated in the atrium. My fingers shook and I wiped a tear from my face now and then.

All of a sudden I heard a group of people walking by me saying Exit, let's go there. Exit, exit, the word was scattered like pearls through their babble. I leaped up and attached myself to them like a tail. They were a group of about ten, with a chubby aunty up front, wearing a T-shirt and track pants, followed by an assortment of family members, teenagers and moms, all leaning together conspiratorially. They know the secret of the exit, I thought, with excitement. Rapidly, they made their way up the escalator to the first floor, skirted around the central shaft to the escalator for the second floor, and once again skirted around the shaft to the escalator for the third floor. It was a lot of fast walking and dodging people to keep up with the surprisingly light-footed group. That fool of a salesgirl was right, I thought, gleefully, the exit *is* on level 3. All at once I felt fresh and quenched by the Diet Coke, my shopping bags now a glad weight on my arms. I even ran a hand through my hair to smooth it down.

On level 3, however, the group paused in front of a small stand-alone shop, discussed something loudly over the music that blared out from it, and disappeared inside. In dismay I stood stock-still. It was a dark, cave-like outlet selling various coloured jeans and metal-studded leather jackets. The name of the shop was Exit.

I looked about me in misery. Clearly there was only one reasonable thing to do now. I must wait till closing time and follow the crowds out—a desperate ploy but the only feasible one.

A uniformed woman tap-tapped by in the orange-and-yellow colours of the mall. Excuse me, I said, what time does the mall shut? It's open twenty-four-hours, ma'am, she said, and went on her way. Where is the exit, I called after her weakly, but she was out of earshot and my knees were buckling under me. Green and yellow lights began flashing around the shop entrance next to me, like a giant marching caterpillar. Night-Bird Sale, a voice boomed from a speaker.

I think this was the point when I began to realize that I was fighting something much bigger than me, something dark dressed up in light. Too much light. Unending light. Here were blue-white tracker lights showing the way to the food court. Elsewhere were pink lights announcing a tweenies sale. A favoured device was white tube light concealed behind sections of false ceiling. All the while the fake sunlight streamed down like God's own creation from the skylight. In the midst of all these varying types of light, there was a light within me that went out, as if exhausted by the competition from without.

It wasn't an all-out surrender, more like a first depression pressed into a landscape. Imagine a flat brown expanse of earth as far as the eye can see, up to the horizon on all sides. Then a small, shallow concave forming on the surface, round, the beginning of a crater. Perhaps caused by a tremor in the earth's crust. Minor pebbles and small stones roll into the centre of this depression. A fairly unobtrusive movement, in one sense, but also the beginning of a pulverization. This is how it was inside me.

On that first night in the mall, I threw up. I have no recollection how long the retching went on, but I do remember simply sitting on a bench outside the restroom, waiting for the night to pass, breaking into sobs from time to time.

In the following days I tried various methods to leave the mall. As each one failed, my attempts became increasingly desultory. People I asked for directions would tell me things like: go to level 9; go down Main Street on level 1; take this escalator up and that elevator down. One uniquely helpful soul told me: the exit is accessed through the Furniture for Fun department store which has its main entrance on the sixth floor and minor entrances on the seventh and eighth floors. The staff was awfully fond of directing me to the elevators. Use only red zone elevators, said one. Another mysteriously referred, one day, to something called the yellow zone, but I never encountered the term again.

The trouble was, the longer I stayed in the mall, the more people avoided me. They hurried away when I tried to stop them to ask for directions. One day, walking past a mirror, I saw how wild-eyed I looked. After that I tried to make regular trips to the restrooms to freshen up and straighten myself out. But I smelled because there was nowhere to shower. Perfume can only mask so much. I bought new clothes now and then, and crammed old ones into the bin. I began to hate the factory odour of new fabric, but there was no way to wash and dry the clothes, so I wore them till my own smell dispelled other smells.

Now and then I borrowed a phone from a shop desk or a customer but couldn't get through to any of the numbers I remembered. The numbers were perpetually engaged. After some months I began to get recorded out-of-service messages. One tantalizing day the phone appeared to be ringing at the other end, but no one answered. I gave up. I phoned the police and told them about my situation. The man enquired whether this was a kidnapping case and I said no. Was it domestic violence? Did I want the women's cell? No, I said, I already told you, I'm stuck in this mall. He made an impatient sound and hung up.

I slept on a sofa in a small storeroom I found in the Furniture for Fun shop (which I had examined thoroughly while looking for its sixth floor exit). It was very cramped, meant only for stocking odds and ends, like lamp shades, textile samples, small bathroom fittings. There was a Xeroxed grid posted on the door, marked by various people in blue ballpoint pen. From this I figured out that the storeroom was accessed only three times over a twenty-four-hour schedule for petty stocktaking and cleaning. But there was a service desk right next to it, so often I had to wait for hours for the staff to take a break before I could slip in and out. Sometimes there were small changes to my storeroom. Once I found a table lamp on a bedside table. I plugged it in and it was almost like having my own bedroom. I lay on the sofa and flipped through a shopping catalogue—there was nowhere I could buy a magazine or book—feeling cozy in the circle of light. The next day the lamp was gone.

Once I attached myself to a salesgirl, stalking her all day. I followed her to the toilet. I sat inconspicuously in her shoe shop while she stared into space. I tailed her as she walked through the displays with customers. At some point she has to go home, I thought, and that's my ticket out of here. I'll simply stalk her all the way out. Many hours later she began walking purposefully out of the store, handbag slung on her shoulder. I jumped up and followed her, hauling my shopping bags along. She walked through the Kitchen King Mega Store and stopped at an unmarked door in a hidden corner. Then she waved an ID card over an electronic lock and stepped through. Wait, I said, and tried to slip in behind her. She turned and looked at me in surprise, and held the door firm. Staff only, ma'am, she said. I need to get out too, I said, with as much hauteur as I could muster. I am unable to find the main exit, and this is an emergency.

Sorry, ma'am, she said, please go to the Main Street on level 2. She began shutting the door.

Are you going home, I asked her wildly, my hand pushing at the door, is it the end of your shift? Let me out too.

Back please, she said, stony eyed. I tried to force the door open against her weight, making desperate noises. She had a small round face, cheap black eyeliner beginning to flake around her eyes and hair pulled back in a bun like a neat airhostess. I could see the pores on her nose. She was very strong. She put her hand on my middle and pushed me hard, looking me straight in the eye. I staggered back and fell, and she pushed the door shut, staring at me as the crack in the door narrowed and closed. I was appalled by this physical assault. I picked up my shopping bags and walked away, trembling. For several days I kept a watch on that unmarked door.

In my purse I found an old envelope. I pushed it under the door, leaving a small triangular corner sticking out. Inside was a wad of cash and a note that said, 'I can give you more money. Please let me out. I will wait here.' The small triangle disappeared. Nobody opened the door for days.

On some days I felt I was witnessing an evil moonrise on a dark planet. I would then sit crouched in a corner, gazing about me with wide, horrified eyes. On other days I appeared to have gathered up the reins during the night, so to speak, and in the morning would go looking for the exit in a most businesslike manner, drawing floor maps on paper napkins, offering bribes, demanding to use the telephone. The staff were polite, firm; when I offered money, they were embarrassed. I trailed other shoppers, hoping to follow them out, but they were either on an endless shopping-cum-eating spree, or they noticed me and told me to bugger off. On many days I simply trawled the racks of goods in a frenzy, buying anything I fancied, using my credit card like a drug. I wept, too. Slowly, however, these wild swings in mood and perspective evened out, and I achieved a sober flatness to my days. I became a veteran of the place, stoic, dry-eyed. I walked the crowds, but I was not of them. I was reminded of the Phantom comics I used to read: The Ghost Who Walks.

But ghosts don't shop. I didn't stop shopping. It was the only thing to do. The winter stock arrived in November and faded away by February. The spring collections began to appear, and

I took some small enjoyment in this coming and going of the seasons. It was change of a kind. I bought a four-wheel shopping trolley made of sturdy canvas in which I could put my purchases, and rolled it along in front of me. Other bags I carried in my hand.

One day I again passed the short, squat woman in her printed sari, trudging along. I decided to talk to her, though I did not see how an exchange with such a person could be productive. I said, excuse me, how long have you been stuck here? Long time, she said. Her grey hair was wiry, gathered in an unkempt bun, and the skin on her face was dry and sagging. This dumpy individual was not the kind of person I would normally want to have anything to do with. However, we were in exceptional circumstances. I noticed she wasn't carrying any shopping bags. What about your shopping, I asked, where is it? I have put it away, she said. Where, I asked. She looked at me with a sly smile, suddenly looking sharp and intelligent. Sorry, I cannot tell you. Places are limited. Places are limited? Do you mean you have found a place to sleep? I asked. No, no, she said, but she was lying. For a moment I had a vision of a dormitory in some hidden corner of the mall, lined with bunk beds. But that was nonsense. She must have found some small stupid storeroom like I had and was afraid I would try to take it from her. How many others are there, I asked. There are others, she said, vaguely gesturing to the mall at large, but they are all wanderers. So are you, I said, and so am I. Yes, she said. I was beginning to get impatient with the fatalistic look of misery that had reappeared on her face. Well, shouldn't we all come together in a group and find a way out? Haan, maybe it is possible, she said. But she looked so unconvinced that she appeared to be humouring me. I persisted one last time. Have you tried to talk to any of the others? I have only seen the couple in the grey salwar and brown shirt, I said, and then there are the two twenty-year olds, but they seem a bit clueless. Arre, there are many others, said the woman, her plump stomach jiggling as she laughed noiselessly. Have you talked to them? I asked. Yes, some of them. And then, apropos of nothing, she amicably said, nice meeting you, and moved on. After that we sometimes exchanged smiles, though it was not often that I saw her or the others.

The piped music, the horrible piped music was getting to me. Every song in the history of music appeared to have been re-recorded either by a hundred-piece orchestra or by a single sad guy with a synthesizer.

However, it was this piped music that gave me the mother of all ideas.

I found myself humming along to a song now and then, entertaining myself by trying to remember the words. I was listening to Olivia Newton-John's 'Heart Attack', murmuring the lyrics while wandering through Juicy Couture. It struck me then that if I faked a heart attack or some kind of medical emergency, I would surely be carried out of here. I was a fool not to have thought of it before, but I happen to be in rude health—it is not a thought that comes naturally to me.

Now I can't simply stand in the middle of the atrium and keel over. I have to choreograph it properly. Having thought it over for a few days, I have made my plans.

Today is the day.

After much deliberation I ditch the rolling trolley, discard the least important of my purchases and tie the handles of the remaining shopping bags together with a piece of string. That way the bags will not scatter and whoever picks them up will bring the lot along. As a precaution I withdraw a good amount of money from the ATM, in case, when I 'wake up', I need ready cash—for hospital expenses, for bribes, for whatever. I have scouted out a location where I will draw the maximum attention to myself: 5 p.m. at the Sale Announcements counter, level 3A. This is where they announce the new sales every day, complete with music, megaphone-wielding staff and, sometimes, confetti. Today I see there is a small troupe of dancers, just four of them, idling on a tiny raised dais, wearing sparkling purple body suits and silver eye make-up.

This is it, I think, gazing at the scene. It's now or never. I plan on creating a real sensation. They will have to carry me out on a stretcher. I notice that two of the staff members behind the desk are holding walkie-talkies. Excellent. An ambulance should be here in no time.

I edge through the gathering crowd as close to the staff as possible, clutching my bags. The press of bodies increases, and music blares out on a high note. The shiny dancers begin their routine, toothy gums on display. Right next to me a member of staff raises her megaphone and begins speaking rapidly, her words an incomprehensible mass of echoes. It is so noisy, such a crush, and I need space around me to have any kind of effect. I jut out my elbows to make room, struggling to hold on to my shopping bags which are very awkward to hold, tied up like that in a jumble. I can't breathe through this stench of human skin and for a moment my feet are lifted off the floor by the momentum of people surging forward. My skin crawls and I scream loudly. I am fainting with fright because the crowd is pressing in on my chest, the woman has trained her megaphone directly into my ear and is letting her voice rip through my head, the dancers are a tangle of cavorting limbs, closing in on me like a glittering and malign purple octopus. I know I am shrieking but I cannot hear myself above the noise. I sink down and fall into a squash of legs and shoes. No one can see me, I will be knocked and crushed by knees and heels, so I try to rise, but I cannot, because I am crumpled on top of my shopping bags. As I scramble up, the fingers that clutch at the bags pull me down again. When I realize this I let go, I unclench my hand, gasping for air, my mouth wide open, my chest wheezing, my throat rattling. Now is the end, I think, and it will come in the colour black. Here it comes. I gulp in black instead of air, and it is over.

ſ

She woke up in a white room with no windows. She was clothed in a white cotton smock. The floor and walls were clean and bare and white. So were the bed, a bedside table, a chair, a cupboard. On the table, a phone. She felt no desire to use it. She lay back on the pillow and, turning her head, rubbed her cheek against the weave of the soft cotton fabric, feeling comforted and at peace. The air was pure. There was not a sound to be heard. It was like waking up in the spa of a space station. She fell again into deep sleep.

When she next awoke, a slim nurse came in wearing a trim white uniform, fitted trousers and a collared top. Welcome to the medical ward of our mall. This is a first-class room. Please let us know if you would prefer class two or class three accommodation, ma'am.

Later a tray of food appeared, and she ate in small bites, chewing slowly, gazing with weak eyes at the texture of her blanket. She slept again.

She slept for many days, waking intermittently to eat and to clean herself in the small white en-suite bathroom. She felt pleasure in walking barefoot across the silent floor, and burying her feet in the lush pile bath mat. She rubbed the white bar of soap on her skin, buried her face in the pure white towels, all devoid of fragrance, all devoid of any demands on her senses. Then she returned to the soft bed to sleep. She felt cleansed, whitewashed, at rest.

They brought her store catalogues as reading material. Now and then she fished in her purse for her credit card and signed for things. She ordered many products. She must, if she wanted to stay here. She understood that. She did not want to think about leaving. Not yet. She was tired, so tired.

Lying in bed, she watched the purchases being brought in and arrayed against a wall, content, like an invalid, to follow movements in the room with her eyes. She left these things alone. Days passed. She did not want anything more. She simply wanted to be left alone, left in peace.

Every day the nurse brought her mineral water in a carafe. So pared down was her life now—bed, smock, food, soap—that she noticed ordinary things with a keen eye. She noticed, for instance, the clear, cool surface of the water as it was brought to her, its liquid disc keeling gently to and fro, perhaps a vanishing bubble or two. This is a lid, she thought, made of the same substance it is meant to be covering. She felt a desire to be like it; self-contained in her own skin. She observed it till it became motionless, then reached out to fill her glass. Odourless, colourless, and cool, the water stared back at her with a round, blank eye. Every day she looked at the water, closed her eyes, and slept. It was the last thing she saw as she fell asleep. It comforted her. She thought of the water as being alive. Sometimes she closed her eyes and imagined the strength of the water filling her. She wanted to be like it, able to be a sprinkle or trickle, puddle or pond, hushed or teeming with life, but always essentially the same; simultaneously a glass of water and a sea. When she closed her eyes, she saw not an empty brown landscape pummelled into craters but a vast pea-green ocean under an arc of sky, quiet but not silent, still but not a watery waste. She opened her eyes and thought, they want to keep me here as an invalid, here on this healing farm or whatever the hell it is; but they cannot, she thought, stop me looking at a glass of water.

She came upon a Malleys catalogue. Inside she saw the perfect pea-green shoes. She ordered them and they were delivered to her room. They stood on the white floor, pristine, green. She felt that if she were simply to slip them on, she could walk out of here. However, she did not yet have the desire to do so. She only wanted to rest. She wanted to be still.

It was days later that she heard a minor commotion. It seemed, at first, like the distant sound of a wailing child, which fell away into other muffled sounds. It was not much, but wedged into her hours of silence it was noteworthy and made her curious. A nurse padded in, mineral water in a carafe. She gazed thoughtfully at the clear water as it came bobbing towards her. Then she enquired, what was that? Almost every day it was a different nurse, emerging from a vast sea of nurses. They were all implacably polite, expressionless. However, she noticed for the first time, beads of perspiration on the nurse's upper lip. This row of beads evaporated almost instantly in the cool air.

Ma'am. A woman. A short woman in a sari. She has no credit card, only a debit card. It is not working even in the third-class rooms. She is leaving now.

The nurse's breathing was heavier than normal. The use of words, information, was unprecedented.

You mean she has to leave, she suggested to the nurse.

The nurse looked at her mutely, her face shutting down, and left.

She lay back on her soft pillows and gazed at the ceiling. She thought of the short, squat woman wandering the mall for another eternity. Till she started looking so beggarly that they would throw her out. She imagined the woman sitting on a bench in the rubbish hold, waiting for someone to mark a Xeroxed schedule with a blue ballpoint, and then exiting in the company of used plastic bags and food scraps.

It is time for me to leave, she thought. But I must play the part. She felt clear-eyed and filled with a stillness. There was a thought in her mind, a notion that felt dew-fresh, like freshly germinated seed. She picked up the phone and enquired about spa treatments. She received a spa menu and a sharp pencil. Running down the options with the pencil point, she ticked the Premium Rose Petal treatment. She was led through narrow white-tiled corridors to a small room. There was a free-standing bathtub filled with crimson petals, a curtained enclosure with a narrow bed, and a salon chair facing a large mirror. She entered the curtained enclosure for waxing, bleaching, a rose oil massage, and scalp and body scrub. Then the rose petal bath, a manicure, pedicure. Her hair was trimmed, blow dried and pulled back from her face, clean and well-brushed. Wrapped in a voluminous robe of soft white towelling, she padded back to her room. The room, with its unmade bed, now had the feeling of a past tense, a point of transit, no more a cocoon. She pulled out the pea-green dress from its folds of tissue-paper. In the same bag she found the bottle of Pigeon Grey perfume and sprayed it into the air, letting its mist settle over her. She slipped into the dress and pea-green shoes, and looked down at herself. I'm still me, she thought. And the shoes are still lovely. But I have discovered something about being like a glass of water.

Once again she picked up the phone. She asked for a

chauffeured limousine and was escorted to an elevator. Her shopping remained behind, massed in a pile against a wall of the room. Before she entered the elevator, a nurse handed her a platinum membership card. Automatically eligible for it without application, having been such a valuable customer, said the accompanying letter. Signature on the back, ma'am, said the nurse, holding out a pen. She signed. Would you like your purchases home-delivered, ma'am? No, stuff them in a pipe and inhale the smoke, she wanted to reply. But she must play the part. With a nod she scribbled an incoherent address and stepped into the elevator. Inside the moving cuboid she felt every pore on her skin come alive, as if each were a separate sensory organ, each one prickling with dread. She felt that she could finally swing past the twisted insides of the mall. But the hideous possibility remained that she would find herself at the Furniture for Fun level. Or the food court.

When the elevator door opened, she found herself opposite the glass doors of the entrance lobby.

As she walked out, and a limousine pulled up, she felt she was facing a scene on a canvas pulled too taut at four corners, yawing out, glossy and plastic. It was the natural light. It disoriented her. A veil of mint-grey was falling over the sky. Twilight. The tricky time of day when pea-green and pigeon-grey work best. She breathed in the humidity through dry nostrils, and felt better.

The scene was strangely empty. The wide driveway curved up to the small artificial hillock onto which the entrance opened. Across the driveway was a vast, silent parking lot, peppered with vehicles. There were no crowds, few movements, the overwhelming mood one of stillness and silence. Five or six palm trees lined the driveway. Two boys kicked a ball around and a girl in a blue frock weaved a tricycle through the tall tree trunks. Some families strolled up from the car park to the entrance, stragglers, licking ice-cream bars and chewing on other food. She looked up at the sky that hung above like a coloured canopy, a sieve through which fresh air might fall. At the moment old breath still hung about her. She climbed into the limousine and inhaled sharply as the door shut, enclosing her in chilled confinement once more.

Driver, she said, to the peak-capped head, please open the windows. I would like some fresh air. The windows slid down. The car rolled off. The breeze touched her face and she leaned forward, looking at everything.

The Girl Who Loved Dean Martin

I live on the top floor of a rundown three-storey London house, divided by the local council into cramped apartments with high ceilings and narrow rooms. The house must be a hundred years old, or at least eighty.

I have now inherited this apartment where I've lived all my life, twenty-seven years of it. There is a tiny attic attached to it, excessively musty, a little wooden cavity in the brow of the house.

Just two days after my father passed away, I begin to go through his things. Wearily, sometimes with a shaking hand. I climb up the rough wooden steps into the attic. Dust particles dance up my nose. A single lamp is set on a low table in a corner. I pull its string to switch it on. It only creates a small circle of light, illuminating mainly itself, like a yellow halo, and I stoop, squinting into piles of cardboard cartons, a mountain of black that melts into the low sloping roof and walls. I prop up a three-legged chair and sit down gingerly. I am taken aback by a pile of vinyl records covered in grey dust in the first box I open. I lift the top few out and sweep my palm across one of the thin paper jackets. It leaves behind a wide moon-shaped arc, and a brown face smiles out at me, black eyebrows raised at the camera.

The title is *Dean Martin Sings For You*. I look at the next one, slanting the large square shape towards the yellow circle of light, and a golden mop glints above a chirpy, cherubic smile, this one's title is simply *Doris Day*, and then Harry Belafonte makes an appearance looking tanned and smug, and a lavish cover of Julie Andrews, angelic and surrounded by red roses and wisps of white lace, and then there are several more of Doris Day.

The shop front of an old record store near Charing Cross station floats into my mind. I will sell these there.

A few hours later, I have not rummaged through even half the boxes. Piles of old clothes and magazines surround me hopelessly, and yet another broken radio and table lamp. All I have done is pull dark pockets out onto the floor—and I have created a terrifying miniature inner-city of black alleyways winding through tower blocks of crumbling paper and cloth. I sink down, my head spinning from want of light and air and I stumble down the stairs for a drink of water.

That night I cannot sleep.

I lie on my narrow bed and stare at a small shape on the ceiling, dark and shifting. Silence dulls faraway street sounds. I turn on my side and stare out at the tops of the other houses in the lane, mostly one-storey structures. I can look down on them and above into the expanse of the London sky. And the sky has forgotten that it is well past the end of summer, that the beginning of autumn must be drawn in by weaving a tent of duns and muted purple-greys, as if setting up a sober but inviting parlour of plump chairs and drowsy herbal teas.

Instead, I think, it is ten at night but those wide chasms slashing through the thick clouds are set on yellow fire.

I root around in my mind: there are some savings, and my fees for the diploma are paid, I must finish it quickly and get a job.

I am only mildly surprised at my calmness, just two days after the event. For I am aloof, dreamy, the inheritor of his temperament. A companionable partnership, I think, neither demanding much of the other. I remember evenings after school; I see him return home from his clerical job, and how oddly the occupation sits on him—for his build recalls a beefy construction worker and not someone who needs to put on a tie every morning; I make him mugs of black coffee till he decides it is time for his half-glass of brandy and supper, and then he falls asleep in his overstuffed armchair, the sundown grizzle on his chin half darkening his face; and I spend the rest of the evening in the dim room, sitting on the worn carpet and leaning against the armchair, hunched over a book and shivering slightly in my red woollen jumper. In the winter we might use the old fireplace and then the pages in my book would deepen with shadows and shades of orange light.

There is an enormous apricot tree in the small square of green attached to the house. For years I have observed the apricot tree with its fruits that ripen every year from hard yellow to soft pink blush, and are never sweet enough to eat. I remember a kiss under that tree. He is rich, he gifts me green contact lenses and says I look so ravishing in them that he will not take no for an answer, and that afternoon he makes love to me hungrily; I emerge out of virginhood in this way, feline and content; but my contentment is temporary, inward looking, it is ensconced within myself, its warmth never touches my occasional lovers who soon leave, disappointed and disappointing.

Leaning out of my window, staring into the bent branches of the apricot tree, I often feel an aperture in my centre: blasts of cold air circulate in and out, they make themselves at home and carve out small cold caves in the four chambers of the heart. I endure this play of the winds and wait for a change, perhaps a warm draught, say from the Mediterranean, maybe the isles of Capri or Santorini, bookish, foreign places of clement humidity where, they say, breezes curl around you like warm, moist embraces. I wait, wide open, for a more temperate clime to find its way in, and this is how I imagine the hollowness in the space where my upper intestine meets my chest cavity, in terms of climate, where different seasons might reside but where now neither spring nor summer has taken root.

My head is still sunk into the pillow. My eyes leave the golden streaked sky, now dimming, and gaze around the four walls of my room. Bare but for two small frames bought at the one-pound bargain shop, dried petalled herbs pressed into gum behind glass. I have the extraordinary sensation that I am peering through the apartment, at its objects muffled in darkness, at the room next door already cleaned and cleared, at the giant boiler holding a silent gargantuan breath before it exhales into gurgles again.

At the broken clutter in the attic.

I wonder when anybody went up there last; how dirty it has all become. Why are there so many old clothes? Why keep broken radios? Why keep old records when there isn't even a record player? Might there, in fact, be one in the mess? Pieces of the bright, smiling faces on the record sleeves come together like a jigsaw, and I think that people looked different back then, that maybe human features have evolved over the past few decades, because I cannot think of anyone now who looks anything like those people; the facial structure was not the same, and they all look so happy, even their happiness looks different. Perhaps it is the cheesiness of Technicolor, its comic book palette, or perhaps it's because their smiles are neither ironical nor provoking, not insolent or confrontational. Just plain old smiling snaps. Old-fashioned words form in my mind like cheeky and gay, and my thoughts will not stop swinging about, now loping towards sleep, now away, into wakefulness.

I am crouched on the edge of darkness.

Suddenly I find that my eyes are wide open and I am seized with a restless desire to go and hunt for the unseen record player. My head swims from standing up too quickly and the wooden stairs are dreamlike as I step unsteadily up into the darkness. I switch on the yellow halo of light again and jerk open the small murky windowpane of the sky hatch. The dust I have raised that afternoon still hangs in the air, like a dotted mist.

I am too impatient to look inside boxes now. What are all these things covered in newspaper and old curtains in this blackest corner of the attic? I begin drawing back the material energetically, with the flourish of unveiling a stage show; dust flies up in puffs and sheets of newspaper float off onto the floor. I grapple with unidentifiable pieces of furniture. I ask myself, *how can this small attic hold all this furniture?* I pause, breathe. My lungs seem to be coated with powdery flakes. I rest, leaning with the palm of one hand on something; I feel it slip and give way. I look down and see that it is a moving circle of felt. I run my palm over the soft felt and the smooth, cubed body and its wobbly arm. I can feel the cold coils of an electric cable dangling against my leg. At the other end of another tangled mess of wires is attached a single speaker. I pick it all up and bring it into the feeble light.

The lamp needs to be disconnected to plug in the player. In the darkness every sound is magnified—the beating of blood in my eardrums, the click of the plug as it settles into the wall socket, the quiet thud of the three-legged chair shifting, and the tentative, spinning whir of the turntable. I fumble with the box of records and slide the first disc out of its sleeve. A violet glow appears through the cramped sky hatch, a kind of dark light, the illumined darkness of pre-dawn. I squat, drop the needle down on the spinning disc, and sit on the floor, my face turned up to the dark square of sky embedded in the sloping roof.

A loud crackling breaks through the dust and then melts into a deep voice, mellow like wood-smoked honey, gentle and heartbreaking as lips against skin. It tells me that I am no one until someone loves me. It is about gold and stars and growing old. It is big band music riding the cracked grooves of the disc, harsh trumpets, scratchy violins and the tippity-tap of a light cymbal swinging the tune along deftly.

My heart stills; I listen closely, straining to swallow each note of the masculine voice into my lungs and stomach.

The song ends and there is a seamless slide into a rasping clattering clacking whirring silence.

Then the voice floats out again, a snappy melody.

Now he sings a song of seduction, how playful, how tantalizing his invitation to fly to the clouds; to sing together and find a rainbow away from the crowds. He switches to Italian; I have no idea what the words mean.

The vertigo of being at the top of a long, steep flight of stairs is now all-enveloping. And the aperture in my centre, where the upper intestine meets the chest cavity, gapes wide because I recognize that the thing I have been waiting for has just wafted in, and there is a lump in my throat, moisture in my eyes, banal, utterly banal symptoms, for it is a stronger emotion than anything I have felt prior to this night of fine dust and dank attic; sitting on the wooden floor I am lifted up by the crackling, warped notes sung fifty years ago and my soul is in danger of being swept up and out through that murky window slanting towards the violet-black sky; I want to step off the roof and float and flail above the abyss, to twirl off into a frenzied dance, to sink to the floor and sob with my face in the rough grained planks, to have the life snuffed out of me, to go up in a smudge of smoke and merge into that languorous, persuasive voice that lazily sways the very air.

Silence falls. A soft crackling begins. It goes on and on, the needle knocking insistently against the circle of paper at the disc's centre; it slides back and forth, makes for the outer circumference, and, finding its way blocked, glides to the centre again to continue its knocking, like a confused animal. I sit stupefied, fingers twisted in my lap. I spy the record cover, I pick it up and lean into the dim glow of the sky hatch; it is the smiling brown face with the raised black eyebrows still looking out at me from the half-moon created by my palm this afternoon.

I turn the record over. There are two more songs on the other side.

The first one is titled 'Come Now to Me'. It feels like an eerie call across decades—a startled yanking, a piston movement begins in my brain and, suddenly, I am afraid. I snatch the cable out of the wall socket and quickly step down into the apartment and into sleep.

After that I feel happier, the next day, the next week, it seems as if a jangling in my head that I didn't know existed has stopped; I return to my secretarial course, finish it in two months, start work at an office nearby, at a company that imports staplers and paper clips from China.

My sudden fear that night in the attic seems foolish, the result of exhaustion; I soon forget it. But I do not forget the emotion the music dragged forth from my innards. I am almost embarrassed at the memory, but then I listen to Side B a few nights later, and then Side A again, and I descend from the attic almost delirious with joy and the head-over-heels feeling of slip-sliding into love, and my chest feels full of laughter, teasingly threatening to bubble out in a vanilla-scented flavour!

Alas, there is only one Dean Martin record in the box. The others don't interest me, I find myself listening to them in a desultory fashion and then one weekend I take them to the old record shop near Charing Cross station and sell them. Disappointingly, the shop has only two Dean Martins in stock, and they give me these and some cash in return for my pile of records. The man behind the counter promises to phone me when he gets 'any more Dean, but they do tend to get picked up right away, love.' I listen to my new Dean records over and over again.

There is a glow in my cheeks that comes from the first flush of love, and I begin to attract the attention of men in the office; but I am in love with another. The women throw me jealous glances but then see that I am unmoved by the hovering, hopeful men and become friendly. There is a small group of them on my floor, a chatty, gossipy bunch of girls who make a beeline for the pub every evening. I find myself increasingly being dragged along with them. They are curious, so curious, about why I have no man; of course, they wouldn't understand if I said I do. I do not tell them that I am indeed in love, that I content myself with listening to his tones and timbres, that he has stolen my soul ever so stealthily via my ear canal, that it is the middle ear, cochlea and tympanum that have become the organs of love, that when his voice rings through the attic I feel exhilarated and alive to all my five physical senses, and sometimes a sixth, seventh or eighth.

It is in the attic that I listen to his songs, sentimental about the place as a couple in love might be about the exact spot where they first met; this sentimental streak in me is an unknown, a surprise, and I allow myself to laugh gently at my self-indulgence. I clear out and sweep the tiny attic and clean the dirt from the skylight which now allows in a remarkable amount of light. A stronger bulb bathes the roof's sloping wooden beams in a soft yellow flush. I carefully wipe the record player with a damp cloth; this reveals an intact and almost untouched casing.

But Claire Willis, assistant to the departmental manager, will not drop the subject of men and finding me one; she is petite and energetic, she has a thick fruity voice, she is popular because of her penchant for loudly saying amusing things. She takes a liking to me, for I am reticent but sunny, and I find her becoming quieter in my company, I feel I soothe her with my self-sufficiency. I am flattered to have an effect on her, it is a great compliment that this loud, popular girl has chosen me.

On evenings at the pub, Claire satisfies herself with her obligatory hullabaloo-ing with the gaggle of girls, and then we chat as a twosome; her voice softens, it becomes lower and more human as she pours out news about her fiancé, Brian, about how they are saving up for a late summer wedding. Mine is the role of listener and I fulfil it well, for I am fascinated at how quickly an hour or two passes in living the details of Claire's optimistic life. She has taken it upon herself to find me a boyfriend, she is mystified at my lack of interest. I'm already in love you know, I say, casually, to brush aside the topic, I'm in love with Dean Martin, he's gorgeous, and Claire shrieks with laughter. We launch into a discussion about men with sexy singing voices; but it is impossible to sidestep the question forever. After I have tried numerous variations of 'But he's no match for Dean' or 'But can he sing like Dean?' to counter Claire's endless suggestions of men I should date, I decide I must tell Claire the truth. I choose a Saturday afternoon when we have planned to meet at a café for lunch and then to walk along the canal to Camden Town.

What about Lu then? You fancy a Chinese bloke? begins Claire conversationally, biting into her sandwich, and I exhale heavily into my coffee. Every girl on our floor has her eye on him, she says, so you'd better snap him up. Melissa Thomas rather likes to think of him as her property, she's half Chinese, you know.

Claire, I begin, and then I stop. Claire looks up at the unexpected silence and stops chewing. I've told you I'm in love with Dean Martin. I am not interested in anyone else.

Claire sits still, looking at me, her jaw tense and full of food.

A troop of raucous teenagers crowds out of the café at this precise moment; the glass doors swing close on the last of them and there is a hush.

She finishes her mouthful and laughs uncertainly, still staring at me. You're not serious, she says, with a half-smile. She says it like a statement, not a question.

I'm in love with Dean Martin, I repeat. I am not a crazy fan, do you hear? I do not live in a room plastered with his posters. I love him. Now can we drop the subject of men forever?

The expression on Claire's face is unreadable; what is she thinking?

He's dead, she says.

I blink as if I have been slapped.

I know, I say, steadying my voice, it doesn't matter. If Brian were to die wouldn't you go on loving him? Or would you forget all about him?

Suddenly, she is on the verge of tears and her high-pitched whisper sounds to me like a scream of rage. How dare you talk of Brian dying! You stupid bitch! How can you compare the two! You're in love with a man who died before you even knew he existed!

What does it matter? What does it matter, Claire? I lean across the table and stare wide-eyed at her, my voice low and urgent.

She looks frightened, her voice shakes, she tells me to see a doctor. A doctor! Then she quickly leaves the café.

In panic I sit watching her small figure hurrying down the street.

After that, at work, there is unbearable politeness from Claire, and there are strained smiles. The women sense Claire's changed behaviour towards me and they follow her lead like a herd of goats.

I begin reading. I absorb the details of Dean Martin's life, the trifles and the glories. I marvel at his childhood as a bootlegger and boxer; how can it be, I wonder, when he sounds like he was born wearing a tuxedo in an Italian vineyard? I shudder at the broken nose smashed in some obscure back-alley boxing ring. I feel my heart singing at his show-stopping fame in the Vegas nightclubs. I am fascinated by the deep bond between him and Jerry Lewis, I am almost jealous, but only briefly, and then, with a laugh, I accept Jerry affectionately as a wife might accept and come to love her husband's inseparable brother or childhood friend. I am full of sorrow at their bitter separation and moved to tears by their reunion, full of gratitude to Frank Sinatra. But I am not swept away by the minutiae of his life. It is his soul I am in love with, his nucleus, distilled and pure, his music; I am in love with his handsome bronzed self, but not with how he lived, how much he drank, how many children he fathered with how many wives; I absorb it all as I read, concentrating, but in the end it does not matter, I feel no desire to go where he was born, to tread the paths he has trodden, to go on a pilgrimage to Ohio, Las Vegas, Hollywood; I am not a fan, I feel nauseated at the thought of joining a fan club, of joining a legion of sun-hatted tourists parading through his old haunts, chattering and clicking their way through the empty shell of his life.

But Italy I feel an affinity for, I begin wishing I could go to

Italy, even though it only produced his ancestors and that lazy, suggestive drawl, but after all that is the important thing: the salty eastern gusts that skimmed over the Adriatic Sea, washing up onto the Abruzzo coast and entering the life-blood of the population, travelling in cells and veins across the Atlantic and taking root in Dean Martin, forming his essence. What is my own essence, I wonder. Possibly the sound of the London Tube, jangling and roaring in underground spirals, riding on dark flinty sparks and dangerous electrical currents, and coming up into glorious air and sunshine, briefly, before plunging into busy darkness again; that's what little girls are made of, I think, completing the nursery rhyme in my mind. But at this precise moment it is irrelevant, because I am gazing at a book in a second-hand bookshop near Charing Cross station, fingering the heavy creamy paper, immaculate square sheets devoted to him, every page crafted individually, divided from the next by a thin sheet of fragile, opaque tissue, each image meant to be unveiled for no more than a few seconds. Dean, candid, brown and sexy in a pool, Dean hard at work in a grainy black and white recording studio, Dean posing against a plain backdrop, a glamorous passport photo; peppermint greens and candy floss pinks from the fifties, sepia stand-up acts in nightclubs from the forties, a whole slapstick section on the grand duet with Jerry, and then just a few of a slightly greying, wrinkled, elegant Dean in the eighties. He is impeccable, I must have this book, but the price is three hundred pounds, absolutely unaffordable and the book is taken from my hands by the irritable shop owner who stows it away again in the shop window. Tribute edition, mint condition, he crabbily informs me.

I dream of saving up to go to the Abruzzo coast; I check the newspaper every week, looking up the listings for the Prince

Charles Theatre in Leicester Square because they show old movies and just occasionally I happen upon a Dean Martin film; mostly I rely on the scant local video library. But it is for his music that I make the real effort, save up money, collect records and CDs. For it is when I hear his pleading, coaxing voice ringing through the attic that my soul presses out against my skin, aching to escape to I don't know where. It is a quiet love, an all-encompassing thing, satiating.

And yet. I am lonely. I am shocked at how utterly abandoned I feel by Claire. I don't dare reach out to anyone for months afterwards. But one day there is a notice up on a board at the local community centre: The Glorious Forties, The Flying Fifties, it says, come and tango, waltz, cha-cha and enter the romance of an age gone by. It is claptrap really, there is no romance of an age gone by, there is romance anywhere you choose to find it, but nevertheless how wonderful to know how to dance to those tunes, to sway. I am excited, I feel strangely stimulated, for after a long time here is an opportunity to partake of the life around me, the life around me that seems to constantly move so relentlessly forward while I seem entirely left out, dead even, till Dean rings in my ears and draws me close.

Just a few evenings later I am trudging through an autumn squall, towards the community centre, leaning forward into a wall of wind.

Behind the heavy swing doors the windy wailing subsides instantly.

I walk along a silent, white-lit corridor, towards a faint clattering, and emerge into a large, noisy, wooden-floored hall. Suddenly, much too late, the embarrassment of having to find a partner dawns on me, and I want to turn around and escape; but here is the instructor, a reed-like man with a hop in his step, he beckons me over and before I know it I am paired off with someone and the instructor is shouting something about 'right foot, one-two-three, back, turn, one-two-three' and I am shuffling along and getting a bit better all the time. When the music comes on I find I am doing quite well, and then he shouts 'quick-change-give-me-passion', in rhythm, like a drill instructor, and off I go across the floor practising with someone else, and what do you know, I'm doing the cha-cha. I walk home with a lilting step, climb up to the attic and lie there contentedly listening to Dean's records, dancing in my mind.

Once a week I walk down the white-lit corridor lined with locked office doors, and emerge into the soft brightness and gaiety of the big hall. I long to dance to Dean's songs and I ask the instructor whether we could but he smiles and says, maybe next time, let's get the steps right first, shall we? And the next week comes and the next, and we begin on the quickstep, and once again I ask him, timidly but persistently, whether we could dance to Dean Martin and he says he has forgotten all about it and will look up an appropriate song to bring with him next time; by the next lesson I am almost in tears because now we are starting to learn the waltz and the instructor has once again forgotten my request.

In despair I retreat to the edge of the group, I want to go home.

And then to my amazement, there are the familiar sounds of a guitar softly twanging out a melody, some long-ago player teasing and plucking the strings and there is Dean's voice caressing the air, echoing and undulating through the wooden beams on the high ceiling, and I see joy breaking out on the faces all around me, surprised grins and slow smiles of recognition that erupt into delighted laughs. I hear the instructor shouting out his pet phrases, 'back to the first lesson', 'we're practising the cha-cha', 'give-me-passion' and I see him busily moving around the bobbing, twirling heads, straightening out, bending and positioning arms and legs, the dispassionate ringmaster of a circus of giant puppets. And all the time Dean's voice envelopes the air with magic and I giggle through the happy thickness in my throat.

Then I notice a handsome young man next to me, he is asking me to join him. He has a sparkle in his eye and an amused smile on his face; he looks straight into my eyes as we dance and I stare back, bewildered, I feel my heart will burst with happiness, and the song is just right, all about violins and swaying oceans and holding me tight.

I'm Diana, I say. Dean, he says, grinning so widely now that I can see his cheek muscles straining towards his ears. I don't understand, I say, confused; really, my name's Dean, he laughs, thrilled like he's delivering the punch line of the greatest joke in the world, and I laugh too, hardly believing my ears. I heard you asking for Dean Martin twice, so I brought a CD myself and put it under his nose and demanded he play it right away; I thought you might like that... His voice trails off and he shrugs. Why didn't you bring one of your own CDs, he asks me after a pause. I...didn't dare, well, I didn't really think I could do that, I say uncertainly, laughing a little, and he looks at me smiling, and pulls me closer to him so that my nose touches his collar and I can smell his aftershave as we sashay across the floor.

And together we dance through the remaining weeks of the course. I can't believe I never saw you before, I say once to him, and he replies, you were in a dream, looking only at your feet, focusing on getting the steps right and then running away before I could say hello to you. Are you always so focused? He smiles questioningly. No, I say, puzzled. Twice we go to the pub after class, where I spend the evening wondering at this turn of events and stumbling, due to lack of practice, as I join words into sentences to make a conversation. I feel as if I am tugging down hard on a paper kite that's diving and looping through the night sky. It is lonely up there, to be sure, and down here is the warmth of the pub with its yellow shade lights and its press of bodies.

Dean courts me the old-fashioned way. He is courteous, holding the door open, pulling out a chair for me. He buys us drinks and won't hear of my reciprocating. He works in a bank, wears a sleeveless tartan pullover and has blue eyes the exact shade of an old ceramic tile above my fireplace. He smells of oranges. I want to travel, he says, as we sit amidst the loud buzz of voices, I am tired of London, where shall we go? I laugh with him because this is our first date and he is being wicked. All right, I say, playing his game, let's go to the Abruzzo coast. He sits back, surprised and intensely interested. Why the Abruzzo coast, he asks. It is Dean Martin's home ground, I say, though he never went there himself. Dean pauses a second, eyebrows raised, and says, wow, you really know this guy back to front, that's pretty wonderful, to be so involved in something. Dean Martin is not a thing, I want to tell him, but I don't because at that moment the ghost of another conversation whispers in my ear and says don't. Not yet. Not now.

He smiles into my eyes, steady and long, and I feel wings begin to beat in my stomach, as if something is about to take flight. A fullness in my chest that makes me happy and hopeful.

One evening he comes back with me to my apartment and we sleep together, the encounter leaving me with a delectable, humid sensation of being simultaneously sated and hungry. It is extraordinary to feel—once again—someone's breath in my ear; it has pushed past the music crystallized there, sidestepping a jewelled minim here, a black gem crotchet there, shouldering past everything and reaching into me like a long, warm arm.

Afterwards, when he goes home, I go up to the attic and look at my records, run a finger over Dean's face. There is a certain silence between us this night. The phone rings and I run downstairs. You left only an hour ago, I laugh. Was it only an hour, he says, it feels like days. I wanted to hear your voice. So I let him hear my voice and we talk till he says, as if to close the conversation, so what are you going to do now? A glass of something? I find it touching that he wants to know. But I don't tell him that I am going back up to the attic.

Men start noticing me again, word gets around at work that Diana has a bloke and the girls, ever so curious, invite me to the pub. I don't go. I spend my time with Dean. The irony of his name is too delicious, I never tire of saying it. At every opportunity I preface my sentences to him with 'Dean...' even when it isn't necessary.

We spend days, weekends and months in each other's arms, in bed, on the dance floor, on the street, fingers, cheeks, arms, shoulders, necks, always touching with affection, lust, passion, through unbroken silences and charmed conversations as mornings crumble into afternoons, half-light fades into sooty blues, and we haven't done and said even half of what we want.

And all the time I have the dreaded feeling that he is in love with me.

It is time, I decide, to take him to the attic, to explain how I feel. It is still a clean, bare space; on the wooden floor only the record player, a pile of records, a rug and a cushion arranged under a soft yellow bulb. The glass of the skylight sparkles clean and polished, the clear night sky peeps in.

This, I say, is where I really live. He gazes around and says it's brilliant. This is you, he says, I love it, clean, simple, sparse, just us and the music. Yes, I say, gladly, but then realize what he has said. I try, earnestly, to correct him—no, it is not us and the music, it is me and the music; I want you to understand, it is not just the music, it is me and Dean... He cuts me off, however, his eyes shining, yes, he says, you and me, and then he kisses me and pushes me down to the floor, onto my rug and my pillow while my stack of records slides gently into an untidy pyramid.

Later, in tears, I scrub the attic clean. I will never bring him here again, this is mine and now it is sullied.

It is only a matter of time till, one day, I cannot bear the open look of love in his eyes. Do you want to live with a cheat, I ask him, and as the words leave my mouth the old loneliness creeps over me. What do you mean, he asks, and my heart shrinks from telling him the truth. I love you, I do, I say. What, then, is the problem, he enquires. He is sitting up now, aware that some disaster is afoot. It is not the kind of love you have for me, I say, in despair, I cannot return your love.

I am in love with Dean.

He laughs at first, then is worried, and strokes my head gently as if I am having an off day. Then as I talk and explain, his face grows frozen, and then the stroking starts up again, as if I am ill, and then the shouting begins. He doesn't give up. He leaves that day, weary and frightened, but returns again and again.

It is Dean in black and white that I always loved the most. Why is it so, I muse, is it because colour is too much of the present, when the person I love more than anyone else in the world is cruelly absent? When I think back, too, it is in scenes of black and white. Claire's sandwich lying forlorn and uneaten when she walks out; the smell of coffee, ever after the smell of desolation; the freeze-dried whip of air in my eyes when I eventually pay the bill and leave, in the tracks of the tiny bobbing figure that has long receded into the distance. The attic, its square of sky, the mist of dust that speckled the air on a night that existed long ago. The smell of oranges when my nose brushes against Dean's evening stubble, the scene where I fail to explain to him that his love is unbearable, suffocating, that it mocks me deeply because it is so intense and true, that I will never be able to return it because I love another, that I cannot live with my insides forever twisted. I fail to explain it because the correct words disappear from my mouth, they go offstage when their presence is the most vital thing, and I have no prompter waiting in the wings. Dean, Dean, why were you not flippant, insincere, a little less in love, I weep. I am relieved when his hurt and angry eyes stop returning to haunt me.

It is Claire's anniversary. She has been flashing her ring all over again at the office, surrounded by glad whoops. That night I stand on Primrose Hill and take in the bird's-eye view of London spread before me. A tattered late light tumbles over the scene, changing the city into a tangle of dim forms and shapes where roofs appear decrepit and houses become small, tumbledown dwellings. The city looks like a vast but temporary settlement. It is ten o'clock and well past the end of summer. And again the yellow chasms in the clouds are like the handiwork of a blowtorch gone mad, leaving gashes of molten gold in a lead-grey sky.

Cotton

It was my birthday the other day. A square envelope of thick, cream-coloured paper plopped through my letter box at about ten in the morning. Inside was a card with a picture of two orange balloons on it. The card said, 'Now that you're 40…' And on the inside it said, '…it's time to have fun!' I was so glad that someone had remembered my birthday that I smiled all morning. I smiled as I put the clothes in the washing machine, I smiled as I sat and sewed in my little tea den. I thought to myself, 'You know what, today I am not going to do anything but bake myself a cake!' I was thrilled with the idea. Maybe I should even put on a nice dress, I thought. So I put on my favourite red skirt with a striped red-and-white top and felt rather festive as I looked in the mirror and smoothed the skirt down over my thighs. Then I went to the kitchen and found a couple of eggs in the fridge. I had baked a great deal of bread over the last few days but luckily, when I opened the cupboard, there was a full pack of flour sitting right in front of my nose. A spoon of cocoa, some sugar, a few drops of vanilla and a stick of butter, and soon I was mixing away. I put it into the oven, and before I knew it, there it was, hot and sweet and delicious. I decided to make icing. I spread it out in a creamy layer over the cake and it looked delightful.

Now I live a very orderly life, I'm not the kind who goes waltzing about town. I find it bracing to look into the fishbowl of the washing machine and see the soapsuds crushing through the clothes and thumping out every last particle of dirt. But I do like injecting a bit of fun into things, so in between my chores I take little detours around the house with a rather amusing duster made of bright pink and yellow feathers, like a long, stiff feather boa. And just like that, the afternoon has slipped away in pottering about the kitchen, making jam or bread or something. And I like a well-made bed, with the sheets tucked in firmly under the corners. It's a must. It's the difference between eating a sloppy sandwich and a properly made one with neat edges. They should both taste the same, but they don't. And one must have a toothpick down the middle to hold all the ingredients together.

But that day, perhaps I was giddy with cake. I didn't get around to cleaning the house properly. And so, before I turned in that night, I saw—oh I have very sharp eyes for that sort of thing—some white fluff on the rug in my bedroom. Horror of horrors, I told myself sternly, young lady, well, not so young any more, you've been so busy having a good time today that you've quite forgotten to do your chores, what about the dusting and the vacuuming? So I picked the fluff off the rug. I used small, hard pinches to make sure I got all of it out.

And then, feeling a tad reckless, I decided to leave a thorough carpet cleaning for the next day. I felt like a stern aunt scolding a disobedient child but I pranced off to bed all cheerful and naughty, and snuggled right in.

Had I known what was going to happen the next day or the next I doubt I would have slept like a peaceful cherub that night.

The next day I was up early, just the same as usual, busying myself around the house. The sun was shining on my houseplants, the sky was blue, and there was a smell of dampness in the air. It's going to drizzle, I thought, a refreshing mid-morning shower, old Mother Nature doing her bit of spring cleaning.

Sure enough, rain began pattering down about an hour later, gentle and steady.

However, it didn't stop.

The soft droplets of water became hard precise pellets, knocking at my windows like a persistent visitor. Soon the world outside turned into a mass of obscure outlines and even these dissolved and vanished. The light was a grey, smoky light, not really light at all. Wet, swirling mists had swallowed up everything. I could see nothing. A gale started up, and the raindrops came down very fast indeed, at a slant. As the wind began to wail, the raindrops began travelling horizontally. I could see them with my face pressed against the glass as I gazed out into the milky grey. They whizzed by as if there were a race track around my house. I was enthralled by this idea, and how funny it would be if each raindrop had a mind of its own, determined to beat the others.

It occurred to me that every raindrop turned into ten as it smashed down. It was like asexual reproduction, each drop a cell infinitely dividing into more and more parts and, good heavens, did that mean we were all going to drown in a deluge of millions of drops of water that had started out only as a thousand?

If each raindrop was a small being, however, each drop that smashed down was on a kamikaze mission. Splat splat splat. Not reproduction but carnage.

Another idea coagulated in my mind. Like egg yolk turning solid with heat. That it wasn't the raindrops that were speeding away from left to right, but my house that was streaking past them from right to left. Hurtling through an astral void, all a vaporous blur outside, save for the little wet stars zipping past me infinitely, but in reality each one a giant—ancient, icy, dead and distant, and it was I who raced past them. I was all alone in the world, all alone, and whizzing past in my solitary ship.

And then, the rain changed direction.

It moved in a mass like a shoal of fish and pointed its nose at me.

Straight at me they came, galactic globes, starscapes, the spawn of countless bubbling single-celled organisms, all hurtled towards me, and I stood protected only by a thin sheet of glass that might crack at any moment under the thunderous assault. The noise pounded in my brain till I could feel and hear nothing else. The glass shuddered violently, and I turned away in fright, wheeling around to look back into my living room. I saw a silent collage of furniture, framed pictures, houseplants and vases. A silent sealed capsule, dry and secure. For a second it terrified me as much as the wild, whipping universe behind me and it was as if I teetered on a craggy ledge, arms flailing, between the vacuum packed contents of my house and the frenzied lashing outside.

I took a cautious step away from the window. Again, I noticed some white fluff. It seemed to be concentrated on the floor under the window where I had stood pressing my face to the glass. There was an armchair near the spot. I went over and examined the chair thoroughly. But no, no tell-tale lumps or bumps or signs of the stuffing leaking out. I vacuumed the carpet vigorously to suck up all the fluff till my arm ached.

That night I slept in fits and starts. The rain did not cease its ferocity. Hard beads of water, emerging out of a wall of mist, shot in straight lines towards every window and bashed at them incessantly. I went to the other side of the house and there too the rain came on steadily in the same fashion. I felt frightened again. How could rain that was moving horizontally towards my north-facing windows, be doing the same on my south-facing windows? Either the wind was moving one way or it was moving the other. It couldn't possibly be sending gusts from all directions towards my house, targeting it. But that was exactly what it was doing. The cacophony was unbearable. In the dead of night I woke and paced around the house, round and round, past all the shadowy windows. The rain was silvery in the gloom, and it was all I could see and hear.

And this morning it was the same. I am going to go down in this deluge, I thought. But the hammering on the window panes no longer had a stupefying effect on me. I shuffled out sleepily from my bedroom—and impossible!—there was more white fluff on the carpet, not just a little this time, but strewn everywhere around my house, like a trail of breadcrumbs cast down by some night-wandering Hansel and Gretel. I stood still and looked at it through bleary eyes. It looked like dirty, white, grainy cotton, the kind that is used to stuff mattresses and furniture. Then something heaved inside me, I can't tell whether it was anger or helplessness. I flung every chair, armchair and sofa onto its side. I checked the upholstery thoroughly, running my fingers and eyes along every single seam, curve and surface, my nose practically touching each stitch. I stripped the bed of its sheets and dragged the mattress onto the floor and examined its topside, underside and every side and corner. I was determined, determined, to find the source of the ghostly white stuff that had confounded me and repugnantly littered my house, I was going to find it and burn whichever article or piece of furniture was responsible. But there was nothing to be found. All was tidily sewn, stitched tight, the stuffing inside neither lumpy nor in danger of erupting.

I even checked all my indoor plants to see if any of them had developed strange buds or seeds that might be discharging the white substance. I was in a frenzy of anxiety. And all the time the rain crashed about my ears.

At about eleven o'clock this morning every piece of furniture was on its side, the curtains hung askew, for I had even checked their hems, and I was close to tears as I surveyed the scene. The universe itself had unleashed a battery of crashing, roiling weaponry to assail me from every side, dirty white stuff was blooming like fungus around me, my home was in disarray and I felt broken. In passing a mirror I chanced to glimpse myself, still in my dressing gown, the ends of the untied sash dangling down from my waist, my hair standing out in wiry clumps and tangles from my bun. My skin dry and flaky and my face an empty, crumpled paper bag. Dismal and wretched. Had I always looked like this?

I was tired and sweaty. My right side itched. I scratched under my arm. I pulled up my clothes and leaned over with my arm raised above my head to examine the spot. I couldn't see anything. Finally I felt it with my fingers. There was a dry scab there. It didn't hurt, but it itched. I went to the full-length mirror in my bedroom for a closer look. It was a most peculiar looking scab. It looked more like a hole. I placed my finger on it and found that I could push right in, it was very roomy. Could it be pus? But it didn't feel wet or sticky. It felt dry and soft and rough, all at the same time. When I pulled my finger out, there was something downy, feathery sticking to it. I then put two fingers in, and pulled out a wisp of fluffy cotton stuffing. My fingers shook with disgust and the cotton floated to the floor. I pulled out a bit more and held it up close to my eyes, almost touching the bridge of my nose...and stared in horror. It was me. I was leaking. Me. Not a piece of furniture. I pulled out more and more of the stuff, it repelled me and fascinated me at the same time. Soon I had pulled out enough cotton stuffing to make a little pile on my bedside table. I roamed about the house, fretting. It was unfathomable.

Questions began occurring to me, strange thoughts that weren't so strange when I thought hard about them. Was I going mad? That was the first question. I was able to answer that one right away. I was most decidedly not going mad, and what was happening was no more a figment of my imagination than the rain frothing on my windowsills. Why am I here, I thought; who or what am I? Am I really a stuffed doll? Am I the creation of a mad scientist who has put me here and stocks my fridge while I am asleep? Has he been putting the recent odd ideas in my head as part of his experiment? Or could his experiment have gone wrong, for here was a technical flaw, a very serious technical flaw indeed. I felt angry, and had a sudden vengeful vision of pulling out all the stuffing from my body and collapsing on the floor like a pillow cover without a pillow in it, so that my creator, whoever he might be, would find me, his creation, punctured, deflated, destroyed, and serve him right. I would slash myself all over so that the stuffing would ooze out, I would go down in a flurry of snowflakes. Could it be snow inside me? What a curious notion. I looked again at the pile on my bedside table. No, it was definitely cotton, the dirty grey-white, grainy kind that you find inside mattresses, not the soft, pure-white, clean stuff sold in pharmacies.

I sat down to think. I badly needed a cup of tea. I went into the kitchen and boiled some water in the kettle. But then a ghastly thought reared its head inside mine. If I am stuffed with cotton, I thought, won't the tea make me go all soggy and limp inside? I stood still in contemplation, in the middle of my kitchen. If I was indeed made of cotton, water would destroy me. From the corner of my eye, furtively, I looked at the waves of water breaking against my windows. Was this The End?

I could no longer remember: had I ever had any tea before? Certainly the tin of tea was there, and here was the sugar. But had I ever used either? Or had I only noted their existence in my field of vision? I looked in the sink, but it was clean, all the dishes washed and put away. I couldn't even remember what my last meal was. Or if I had ever had a meal.

I opened a kitchen cupboard. To my wonder, it was full of jam jars, all neatly labelled, dozens of them. I couldn't remember ever tasting any.

I felt I must phone someone, ask for help. But who should I phone? I could not think of whom to phone. I paced about the house, fidgeting and twisting my hands together, and not coming to any decision. Now and then I stopped in front of the mirror to examine the hole. What could have caused it? Funny, it didn't hurt at all. That was fortunate. I examined other parts of my body but found all in order. There was some fluff under my toenails, but I couldn't tell whether it was seeping out from there or whether it had just snagged there as I walked barefoot around the house. The sofa and all the chairs were still on their sides. I must put them right, I thought. But still I paced, paced, paced.

Slowly, I began to calm down. I washed my hands and noticed that they didn't go limp like a soggy rag. Obviously I was covered with some kind of waterproof material. The things you hear about nowadays, all this new-fangled technology is beyond me, I tell you. In another twenty years we'll be flying around our houses, not walking. Human ingenuity is a remarkable thing, really.

I started tidying up the house. I even opened one of the windows very slightly because it was getting stuffy inside. The rain, of course, squeezed through, and a small puddle of water began forming below the window. Well, I'd wipe it up later, I needed some oxygen, I was feeling suffocated. A wet puff of air ran through the house. And then my insides cramped with fear because I saw my little pile of cotton stuffing on the bedside table begin to scatter. It was being blown away bit by bit. No, no, no, I screamed, as I whipped around towards the open window and slammed it shut. The room became still again, vacuum packed, airless and safe. I padded back to the bedroom and gathered up all the bits of cotton between my palms. How stupid, stupid, stupid, to leave them lying around like that. Once again I stood with my side to the full-length mirror, and stuffed the cotton back in, holding little wads of it between my thumb and forefinger. But how could I plug the hole? I could not think how. So I decided to leave it for the moment.

I went to the sofa and turned it back on its four feet amid the dark wreck of my living room. All was illuminated only by the silver-grey light which penetrated through the dull, wet windows, and now by the flickering shadows of the television screen. I didn't want to miss my favourite show. It was still just the commercials, and they drowned out the thumping of the rain rather effectively, till it was just a steady drumming in the background, just another boom boom boom. A flurry of cotton emanated from my side as I flopped down on the sofa. Here was a puzzling problem, how was I going to solve it? I couldn't just go on losing cotton. No matter, I thought cleverly, I've found the solution. There was a good sharp fruit knife that had fallen off the coffee table in front of me. I picked it up and slashed at the sofa seat. I pulled out some of the cotton stuffing and inserted it carefully into my side. As I watched, my hand wandered to the gash in the sofa seat and slid inside. It felt snug and cosy there. Just fine, in fact.

The House on the Hill

The little girl ran up to the great white house on the hill. It was the last house, the one furthest up. It was ensconced in an alcove of trees. The criss-crossing arcs of heavy-leafed branches revealed only glimpses of the whitewashed walls until a certain corner was turned and the house suddenly sprang into view. On grey days, swathes of clouds swarmed above the house, billowing out in dusky pigments of charcoal and slate and ashen-blue, forming a towering backdrop and circling endlessly overhead. But today, like most days, the sunlight twinkled down from a blue sky over the thickets of drooping bamboo and nodding boughs of sprawling gulmohar trees. It glanced off the sloping russet roof and danced through the trim blades of grass.

The girl couldn't have been more than thirteen years old, but she was sharp and attentive. She had been working in the house for a few months now, and found it a relief to run up there in the morning sunshine every day, away from the cramped room in which she lived with her parents, three sisters and baby brother.

Below the hill, well hidden from view, were several such rooms in which the labourers lived with their families. During the day they would toil at building the houses that had started dotting the small hill, and at dusk they would walk down again to their ramshackle dwellings.

As she ran, the wind caught at her long purple skirt, puffing it out like a cloud, and as she neared the house she slowed down to adjust her golden paisley nose ring. It was a cheap one, and its ruby-red stone was only a piece of glass. But its effect was striking against her smooth, dark skin.

In the mornings she would sweep the great hall where she had once marvelled at the white marbled floor, the dark wood and heavy silks of the furnishings. She marvelled no longer, but continued to revel in the cool high ceiling and wide glass windows through which streamed light and air in ample quantities. Then she would go upstairs into the bedrooms. She folded the clothes in the master's bedroom, made the bed, drew back the curtains, and swept the floor. There was never much dust to sweep out. The master was a fine-looking man, very tall and handsome even though he must have been at least sixty years old. He spoke to her kindly and asked if she was tired with all the work. Sometimes he would ask whether she was learning her alphabet and always chuckled softly when she said yes.

The master had a daughter who made the little girl feel shy when she smiled at her. The girl would look wonderingly at the young mistress's radiant smile and long dark hair. Now and again the young mistress would softly ask the little girl to hand-wash some delicate piece of clothing, a scarf maybe, or a blouse, made of fragile, beautiful fabric. Her room was often in disarray, scattered with possessions and always filled with a strange, lilting music, alien and enchanting to the little girl's ears.

The master's wife was dead and so there was no one to look carefully into the running of the house. And yet the household ran smoothly. The only noise created was by the people who were often invited to the big house for feasting and drinking, among them many men who guffawed deeply and women who stepped in like glittering birds.

The master and his daughter came and went gracefully from the house, going about their engagements in town. Often the little girl had no work all afternoon. On such days, she would sit by herself on the sunny patio facing the garden; a pair of jacaranda trees swayed on either side of the speckled cream floor and a warm zephyr always seemed to rustle through the yellow buds and lime-green creepers growing on the wooden trellis which covered the patio. No one knew what she was thinking as she gazed at the expanse of green grass and at the white and crimson bougainvilleas that twisted and turned along the fence at the far end of the garden. Only occasionally the cook would gruffly tell her to stop sitting idle and help with washing the dishes. The little girl didn't mind, for most of the time no one disturbed her reveries on the cool, cream patio floor.

On some days, at least thrice a week, the master's secretary would call out to her to bring her book of alphabets and the little girl's face would light up with pleasure. Her head bent over the book, she would haltingly read aloud with gentle prompting from the young secretary. She had been delighted on being presented with clean, new books, and had turned the pages fervently, looking at the letters, wishing she could remember what they spelled. She felt stimulated, and began to recall long-ago school lessons. Now the covers were dog-eared and frayed, and she knew how to read most of the words inside.

Though the master usually spoke very little, he had much to say before guests came for dinner. Then he would stride about the great kitchen, ordering the cook to do this or that. On this particular evening, the master was very busy. There was to be a coal fire lit in the garden, and meat was to be cooked over the open flame. The winter months were setting in, and the weather had turned chilly. A large table was set up on the lawn and covered with a deep red tablecloth. Eight place settings of blue and white porcelain were arranged on the table. The silver cutlery gleamed faintly in the fast approaching darkness, and then sprang to life and sparkled as tall blue candles were lit all along the centre of the table.

Soon the guests arrived and there was much clinking of crystal and pouring of drinks amid the murmur of conversation. The evening grew gayer and voices rose higher as the coal fire was lit, fanned and stoked, and the pieces of roasted meat transferred to the table by the uniformed bearer. The little girl had stayed on this evening because one of the maids was away, and now she ran back and forth between the kitchen and the garden, carrying all manner of things. An extra blue napkin, neatly folded into a cone. A jug of water. Tall thin-stemmed glasses and small trays of freshly fried aubergine and green chillies. Once, as she left the table to run into the kitchen, she felt that the party might be talking about her, but she couldn't be sure because, for the moment, they spoke in English. She hoped they were praising her swiftness in bringing them what they wanted, and the thought made her hurry about her work even more, paying close attention to the master's face and the young mistress' smile. She wasn't tired at all, but a small part of her mind reminded her that soon she, too, would taste the delicious dripping meat in the kitchen, with the cook watching over her.

As the little girl stood by the bearer holding a hot skewer, a pearl-faced lady arrived, walking quickly across the dimly-lit garden, all billowing silk and golden tassels, like a delicate ivory ship sailing over a dark green sea. Her arrival created a sensation;

how extraordinary she looked, they all said; how her skin glowed; how heady the air was with her perfume. The quiet silks of the others paled before her and they all wanted to know where she came from, so gorgeously dressed. The master, expansive and welcoming, declared himself honoured that she had left what was no doubt an important occasion to grace his table. It turned out that the lady had been to a great society wedding—but what a bore it had been, she said, tossing her head so that the diamond drops in her ears quivered dew-like in the candlelight. She was all agog with the gossip; the presents on display; a certain silver samovar that was whispered to be hundreds of years old and still in the family—she had seen it herself this night; the fairy lights in the trees designed to resemble cascades of shimmering water; the evening had been beautiful, but such a bore. The little girl, busy with her tasks, strained to catch as much as she could, filled with wonderment at being within breathing distance of that golden world. The meal, almost at an end, was revived by the lady's entrance. She spoke with her copper-brown eyes as much as her rose lips, and all banter now centred on her. The bearer frowned into the embers and began hastily roasting fresh skewers of meat.

At the height of the laughter, amid the last emptying plates, the master rose and strode indoors. The spell was broken. As if mildly stunned by the amount of food they had eaten, the guests fell silent and looked at him as he walked away, smiling at each other. The lady sank back into her seat, pursing her lips into a dry pink petal as the attention fell away from her.

Puzzled, the little girl followed the master to ask what he needed, but he was already in the kitchen. The cook stood over a deep blue dish. Piled up next to it were a dozen yellow bananas sliced lengthwise into long halves. As the master instructed the cook to arrange the slices carefully in the dish, the girl realized that the old woman had never made this preparation before. A cup of chopped cashew nuts was sprinkled over the bananas. Next, thick swirls of sweet honey. A large bowl of warm milk was brought, a pinch of saffron stirred into it, and the mixture poured evenly over the fruit. The dish was placed in the heated oven, and soon the little girl was walking with mincing steps over the lawn, balancing the hot dish rather clumsily in her hands, now clad in thick cotton mitts.

The guests' faces lit up with smiling curiosity, and the master was in high spirits. All sorts of questions were asked about this new arrival, and the gleeful voices grew louder as the master picked up a large long-handled ladle and poured into it, from a glittering swan-necked bottle, a translucent liquid the colour of deep amber. He held the liquid-filled ladle over the wavering tip of a candle flame, and warmed it well. A feminine squeal was heard. The sound had emerged from the beautiful woman who sat erect and expectant, her long pale neck like polished marble. A match hissed and flared, the master touched the warmed liquid with the match, and all at once it seemed as if he held in his hands a ball of fire. The jagged blue flames ran amok on the amber liquid, licking at it and trying to set themselves free of the constricting half-globe of the ladle. Swiftly, the master tipped the ladle over the dish, and the blue flames tumbled down. The ball of fire, now mad with release, devoured the chopped nuts and slices of fruit before dying out, satiated. Again, the lady squealed, almost screamed, and a satisfied 'ahh!' ran around the table.

An exquisite smell emanated from the dish, and the master added another splendid splash of the amber liquid to it. There was a clatter of spoons as the master's daughter served out portions and the guests began eating. The little girl, who had watched the proceedings with amazement and delight, now heard clearly what they were talking about. They spoke of many things, other things. Incredibly, the miraculous fruit preparation had already been forgotten, and one by one the guests laid down their spoons and pushed away their bowls, leaning back in contentment.

The little girl ran back to the kitchen. She felt awed by the dazzling ceremony she had just witnessed in the dark garden, though the feeling dissipated somewhat under the bright lights of the kitchen and the cook's terse order to sit in the corner and wait for her dinner. Soon, the staff were sitting in a circle on the floor and noisily eating the generous amounts of meat and vegetables that remained. Sounds of mirth and stories being recounted floated in faintly from the garden. The girl sank her teeth into the savoury meat and ate her fill, only half listening to the bearer's voice complaining that his white uniform had coal stains on it. She felt tired now. Her legs ached and she suddenly wanted nothing more than to walk back down the hill to her father's hut. She noticed, with surprise, that the blue dish with the bananas had appeared on the floor along with the plates of meat and vegetables. The fruit lay in a pool of milk with a few delicate strands of saffron clinging to the long slices. There was enough for everyone to have a small helping, and the girl happily accepted her portion anticipating, with a thrill, delicious, sweet morsels from the strange, grand dish. And, yes, the fruit had soaked up the saffron milk and turned soft and juicy, and the cashews had turned satisfyingly crunchy. And everything was suffused with an edgy, biting aroma that was unfamiliar, warm and pleasing; as she scraped the last of her portion from her plate, she thought it must be because of the mysterious golden-amber liquid. The meal over, the staff turned to their last tasks of the day, their movements now slow and weary.

Sleepily, the child drained her mug of water.

'May I go?' she asked the cook.

The old woman nodded without looking at her and said brusquely, as she usually did, 'Make sure to be on time tomorrow.'

Running out to the gate, adjusting her nose ring, the girl passed the garden, and heard the master and young mistress calling out to her. She hurried over to where the guests still sat, sprawled out on their chairs. She overheard a man saying in a low voice, 'Yes, she must be tired, running back and forth like that. She's only a child.'

The master watched her approaching, and when she stood in front of him, he asked with concern, 'Are you tired?'

The girl shook her head shyly.

'But you've been running around all evening.'

She didn't say anything. She was half-happy at the kind words, but she was tired and wanted to go. Everyone's eyes were on her.

'Did you have your dinner?'

'Yes,' she replied, in a clear voice.

'What did you eat? Did you have the meat?'

She nodded and said, 'Yes.'

'And did you like it?' There was a note of kindly amusement in the master's voice that broadened into a smile when she nodded.

There was a movement from one of the chairs and a slight murmur. The handsome lady had shifted in her seat and was looking around the garden, bored with this interrogation. Suddenly she turned and said, brightly, 'What about the dessert? Did you have the dessert, child?' She used the English word for 'dessert' and the girl hesitated, frowning slightly.

At once the master said, 'Yes, what about the fruit? Did you have some?'

'Yes,' said the girl, beginning to smile.

'Good,' said the master as if to finish the interview and turn back to his guests, but he was drowned out by the woman.

She gave a loud peal of laughter and covered her mouth with the palm of her hand, saying, 'Oh, don't tell me you gave her the fruit with the brandy! She's had the brandy!' The lady glanced around comically at the other guests. She was determined to make the most of this one last amusement of the evening. The child was confused, she did not know what brandy was. She had liked the dish a great deal, and was puzzled as to why this lady was laughing. And when she saw a stern hardening of the master's face, dread and fear overtook her. The master shook his head and said something in English to the lady, whose laughter subsided at once. She sat back as if chastised. The child heard someone say very softly, 'Yes, don't tell her that.' But she didn't know who it was. It might have been the young mistress.

'You can go home now,' said the master, with forced joviality, as if to pretend that nothing had gone wrong.

The girl walked slowly down the hill. The clouds had built themselves into a teetering tower overhead, and a steady wind was gathering force. The moon was a small silver chunk in the night. Gusts of wind whipped around the girl's long purple skirt, making it flap and beat against her thin brown legs. She felt a profound sadness. But she did not know why and, had someone asked her what the matter was, would not have been able to explain.

Drinks at Seven

Pradyumna rifled through the drawer in his study, looking for the bottle opener. Padma came in. 'Chanda and Lalit are coming for drinks in half an hour. And you haven't changed yet.'

Irritated, Pradyumna said, 'I know they are coming. I invited them. I told you they were coming at seven. It only takes me two minutes to change. I don't need two hours like you. I'm looking for the bottle opener.'

'Which bottle opener?'

'The one Lalit gave me last week.'

'What does it look like?'

'I showed it to you. It's long and flat and shaped like a woman's leg.'

'You didn't show it to me.'

'I did. It's long and the leg is slightly bent and she's wearing one of those high-heeled sandals. Silver.'

'He gave you a silver bottle opener?'

'It's not really silver. Have you seen it?'

'Go take a shower,' said his wife. She walked out, yanking her T-shirt off over her head.

He entered the TV room twenty minutes later exuding a

strong spicy scent, his hair and neck and palms still damp from the steam of the hot shower. 'Padma, find the bottle opener, yaar.' She had changed and was flipping through a magazine.

'For God's sake, use another one. Look in the bar.'

'But I want to use that one,' Pradyumna insisted. 'Lalit brought it specially from Hong Kong.'

'Weird, bringing a bottle opener from Hong Kong.'

'For God's sake, stop reading that fucking magazine. Where are the snacks?'

'In the fucking grill, grilling themselves.'

'God knows why you read *Good Housekeeping*. You don't even like housekeeping.' His voice trailed off as he walked out. She narrowed her eyes and tossed the magazine on the sofa with a sharp flick of her wrist.

She heard Pradyumna looking through the drawers in the bar cabinet. Then she heard the slamming and sliding of more drawers being opened and shut as he rummaged through the sideboard in the dining room downstairs. She leaned over the railing and looked down at the top of his head. It was a full head of wavy hair, like that of a nineteen-year-old. The bloated belly rather gave it away, of course. And then there was the square, squat box of his chest and shoulders, threatening to make him look like a giant toddler. He was mentally nineteen. Looking for a ridiculous bottle opener shaped like a woman's leg. She idly imagined dropping something heavy on him from above. She went downstairs and leaned against the dining table, her weight on one hip, watching him.

'A bit juvenile, don't you think?'

'What?'

'It's like one of those adolescent fantasies. Grab a woman's leg and open a bottle of booze. What was Lalit thinking?' Pradyumna ignored her. 'Does Lalit know that Chanda sleeps with that guy from her office when he's in Hong Kong?'

'What?' Pradyumna straightened up and stared wide-eyed at Padma.

Padma giggled, and looked superior. 'Oh yeah, baby. While you kids play with your toys, the girls are out getting the real thing.' Then she said, 'For God's sake, don't say anything to him.'

Pradyumna looked like he was going to speak, but then remembered he was searching for the bottle opener. He walked to another chest of drawers and started opening them one by one.

'Don't be a fool,' said Padma, 'use the other bottle opener.'

Pradyumna shouted, 'Damn it, my friend has given me this thing, and I want to use it when he comes here for a drink. Okay? You haven't bloody well lifted a finger to find it. At least keep track of the things in your home. Instead of finding out who's screwing whom. Supervise the servants instead of reading about good housekeeping. Throw out some of your rubbish, some of your hundred purses and two million shoes. I can't find a damn thing in the house when I need it.' He was shouting so hard that his chest and shoulders bent forward over the bulge of his stomach. His eyes were savage under his mop.

Padma started speaking calmly but her voice rose and she ended by shrieking out her words. 'What would you do, Pradyumna, if I told you that *I* was the one sleeping with some guy? Would you care, or would you go on looking for your fucking bottle opener?'

'I would go on looking for my bottle opener. Okay? Are you happy? Is that the right answer?' Pradyumna spoke softly and matter-of-factly, and his small plump lips wore a sneer.

The doorbell rang. There was a silence.

'Fuck. I still haven't found this thing.'

Padma walked with quick steps to the door and twisted the doorknob open. Lalit and Chanda wore cheerful smiles. Very cheerful and very fixed, and both gave a wary glance over Padma's shoulder. Padma produced a charming smile, somewhat martyr-like. Lalit, tall and fit with neatly combed, grey speckled hair, at once launched into his usual act; flamboyantly he bent over at the waist and kissed her hand, flinging wide his other arm at the end of which dangled a bottle of expensive wine. 'My lady,' he said with breezy exaggeration, while Chanda filled the air with hilarity and declarations of *how slim* Padma was looking, and *where* did she get those shoes, *yaar*.

Inside, Pradyumna turned on the sound system, and a raspy jazz crooner took over.

'How's the international tycoon?' bellowed Pradyumna as Lalit strolled into the living room followed by the two women.

'Give me a break, man,' said Lalit, grinning, but his walk became a loose-kneed swagger as he went over to Pradyumna and clapped him on the back.

Padma raised her eyebrows at Chanda in playful, theatrical admiration. 'Kya baat hai, Chanda, international tycoon and all.'

Chanda flopped down on a sofa, exaggerating a what-international-tycoon-someone-give-me-a-break look on her face. 'Pradyumnaaaa! Driiink!' she cried, puckering up her mouth and forehead, and pretending to shout.

'Chanda, saali bevdi!' said Pradyumna, his round shoulders heaving with chuckles. 'The usual, sweetheart?' He started mixing her a concoction.

Lalit handed the bottle of wine to Pradyumna. 'Dude, rice wine. Ever had any?'

'The Chinks have rice wine, right?' said Padma, with interest.

'So do the Japs,' interjected her husband authoritatively, with an eye on Lalit for confirmation.

Lalit assumed a patronizing air, and stood with his feet planted slightly apart. He waited for quiet in the room as Pradyumna handed drinks to the women, and then spoke slowly, pedagogically, his head tilted to one side, looking at the carpet with serious concentration. 'This rice wine, Padma, Pradyumna—and, Chanda, you listen too, this is interesting,' he added in a pompous aside to his wife, 'this is Japanese rice wine. You would know it as sake. There are two basic types of sake. Futsu-shu, which is regular sake, and Tokutei meisho-shu, which is special designation sake.' They all glanced at each other with a knowing, cosmopolitan air. Pradyumna looked rather struck by the elegant, unfamiliar words rolling off Lalit's lips so casually.

'The wine I have brought for you, Pradyumna,' continued Lalit, gravely, 'is special designation sake. It is pure rice wine, made from fermented rice. No additional alcohol has been blended in, it is absolutely pure. This one is called Junmai Ginjo, it is dry and mellow and quite superb. Padma, it is a premium quality wine, made from highly polished rice.' He waited, supremely superior, for Padma to ask him what highly polished rice was.

But Chanda interrupted like a chattering monkey. 'You know, they polish away almost all the outer husk of the rice, and then make the wine only from the kernel. That's the best kind of sake.'

'Chanda...' murmured Lalit, with an irritated smile, as if reprimanding her for taking such a simplistic view of matters. She was blithely eating a cashew nut.

'Thanks, man,' said Pradyumna, looking respectfully at the frosted bottle. 'I'll put it in the fridge. Listen, I got hold of those cigars you were telling me about. Ashwin was going to pass through Miami so I phoned him in LA and said, bastard, at least pick these up for me from your contact. He came back only yesterday.' Lalit looked suitably impressed and interested, so Pradyumna hurried inside to fetch them.

The wives leaned back, clasping their drinks, and looked at each other. Chanda's thin frame was stick-like among the oversized sofa cushions. Padma smoothed her top over her waist and glanced down to check that no surprise bulge was visible.

'So?' said Padma, but then couldn't think what to add. 'All well?'

'Going on,' said Chanda in a bright voice, aware that they needed a topic.

'Heard about Zoonie?' said Padma.

'I know,' said Chanda, eyebrows raised.

Padma waited a few seconds till Pradyumna stepped back into the room and then called out to him, 'What was the name of Zoonie's lover?'

Her husband looked at her impatiently. 'Rick.'

Lalit, now curious, was moving towards the women. But there was no more information forthcoming from his hostess about Rick and Zoonie's amour. Instead, she said, 'I've got to hand it to her, though, slut that she is. I mean she goes out there and takes what she wants.'

'What about her husband?' asked Lalit.

'He's one of these finance types,' said Chanda. 'All paunch and no play.'

'That sounds familiar,' said Padma. 'Who can blame her?'

Chanda stared, fascinated, at Pradyumna who was standing with his back to them, fiddling with the box of cigars on the bar.

'Ashwin got these at a discount, man,' said Pradyumna, grinning at Lalit. 'I know someone who paid almost double for these.'

Chanda turned to look at Padma, her fascination unabated, as if she had suddenly discovered something highly interesting. A servant appeared with a plate of kebabs and set it down on the low table where the women were lounging on sofas. The room was lit with the yellow glow of various silk-covered table lamps.

'I mean, it's not like Zoonie was being terribly subtle or anything,' continued Padma loudly. 'It was all happening under his nose.'

Lalit walked over to the box of cigars but then changed his mind and loitered in the middle of the room, drink in hand.

'But what would you do if you knew your husband or wife was having an affair?' asked Chanda, with a gleaming smile, 'I mean, the first thing that comes into your head is that you'd walk out. But it's never that simple, is it?'

'It's difficult for a woman to just walk out,' said Lalit, shaking his head. Pradyumna's eyes suddenly registered the conversation when he saw that Lalit was participating in it. He pulled a bar stool closer to the cluster of sofas and perched himself on it.

'That's just the problem,' said Padma triumphantly. 'You're assuming that it's the man having an affair, and that the woman will find out, and then have to decide whether to walk out or not.'

'That's the most likely thing, isn't it?' said Pradyumna. He winked at Lalit, but Lalit missed it.

'Well, then, what about Zoonie?' said Padma at once. She sat up straight, neck out and shoulders back, ready for a debate.

'Zoonie's a slut,' said her husband, and got up to change the CD. 'Chanda, have some kebabs, yaar, I told our Jeeves to get them especially for you.'

'Mmm, I love kebabs from Lucky Mian,' said Chanda, reaching for another one.

'Lucky Mian has been around for fifty years, haan,' said Lalit, impressed, though he and everyone else was well aware of the fact.

Padma leaned back, her lips twisted into a little beak, and then got up to fix herself another drink. Chanda watched her with small dark eyes, much entertained. She stretched out a limp arm towards Pradyumna, dangling her empty glass with her fingertips, and looked at him, beseeching and flirtatious. He jumped up, chivalrous and eager to refill it. They were all throwing back their drinks now.

'Pradyumna tells me you've introduced him to a lady. Or should I say a lady's leg,' began Padma, a while later, during a lull in the conversation. She said it with a straight face, but deliberately twitched her mouth, as if she might dissolve into laughter at any moment.

Lalit looked baffled, and then his face cleared. 'Oh yeah, ha ha. Where is the lovely lady, yaar?'

Pradyumna winked at him. 'In my bedroom.'

'Does that mean you're still active in that department, darling?' said Padma.

'That shows how much you know,' said Pradyumna, winking now at Chanda.

'If I were the suspicious type I'd say you were making a move on Chanda,' Padma said, rather tipsy now. 'Eh, Chanda? Or did you wink at my husband first?'

Chanda smiled politely. Lalit gave a shrug and made a comic face at Pradyumna.

'Don't be stupid, woman,' said Pradyumna, and turned to Lalit. 'Switch to whisky soda?'

'What are you going to open the soda with?' hammered on Padma. 'Do you know, Lalit, my husband has lost that silly woman's leg you gave him. And he won't use any other opener. He thinks he's under some obligation to use it every time you come over for a drink. Ah, the innocence of friendship. That's true friendship, I tell you.'

'Lost it?' said Lalit, raising his eyebrows at Pradyumna.

'I haven't lost it, yaar. It's here somewhere.'

'Let's play a game,' said Chanda, with a little snigger. 'Let's all look for the lady's leg. What a lucky lady, to have so many people looking for her. Like in *Desperately Seeking Susan*. Ha ha.'

'Desperate is right,' said someone.

'First of all, we need some candles, because it's more fun in the dark.'

Padma walked away a little unsteadily to get them, holding her Bloody Mary in a tight grip.

'What's this, what's this?' said Pradyumna, all jovial now.

'What's the prize for finding it?' asked Lalit.

'Well, let's agree on something,' Chanda said.

'Okay, whoever finds it gets to sleep with my wife,' said Pradyumna, swaying a little. 'I have the advantage, I know where it *isn't*. Though now I'm not so sure I want to find it.'

'You're sick,' said Padma from the door of the room. She stood leaning against the door frame. 'God, I hope you don't find it. And what if I find it, moron? Am I supposed to sleep with myself?' She cackled, somewhat hysterically.

'No, then you get to choose who you sleep with,' interjected Chanda, grinning.

'What if Chanda finds it?' said Lalit.

'Then,' said Padma, collapsing onto the sofa in a fit of giggles, 'we'll be a lesbian duo.'

They were all sprawled out on the sofas and chairs, laughing at their own absurdity. But Chanda recovered first, and sat silent while the others coughed and wiped their eyes.

'What if Lalit finds it?' she said, when everyone had piped down.

'You're not serious,' said Padma.

Pradyumna looked disbelieving too. 'Sweetie, it was a joke. Padma isn't really the prize.'

There was a short silence. Lalit looked around the living room with great interest as if searching for a hook on which to drape a new topic of conversation.

'You're the one who suggested it,' said Chanda, defensively.

'I didn't. You're the one who suggested the game. I joked about the prize. Think of another prize if you still want to play this silly game.'

'On second thoughts, I don't necessarily want people poking around the drawers of our apartment,' said Padma.

They all stared at Chanda, who looked embarrassed but stubborn. Her chin jutted out, and she suddenly seemed like a small, spiteful child cornered in the playground. She spoke slowly, and enunciated each word clearly. 'You know,' she said, and she looked from her husband to Padma and back again. Her husband sat very still. 'How do you know they haven't slept together already?' she said, turning to Pradyumna. 'How do we know, Pradyumna, how do we know?' Pradyumna stared at her.

'I am not sleeping with Padma.' The dry, tight words leaped out of Lalit's mouth, leaving him looking stricken. The air, which had been fluid with a general bewilderment a moment ago, congealed into something concentrated, perilous. Chanda looked around at them all.

Suddenly she threw her head back with a peal of laughter. 'Don't be silly, yaar, I was joking. Just look at your faces!'

There was a collective slackening of the tension in the room and a twittering sound from Padma. Lalit picked up his chilled glass and took a sip.

His wife plumped up the cushion behind her and sat back, straightening her spine and rearranging her skirt over her crossed legs expectantly, as if a new guest was about to enter the room.

'Well...we're not,' said Lalit warily after a few seconds. Chanda looked at him with contempt.

'Not what?' said Pradyumna with a lopsided grin that faded as soon as it appeared. His attempt at a laugh came out merely as an expulsion of air.

'We're not sleeping together. Just to clarify, you know.'

'I know that,' said Pradyumna.

'I know you know that.'

'Then why say it?'

'Just to, you know, clear the air.'

'Oh dear, how foggy the air seems,' said Chanda, staring wide-eyed into the middle distance.

Lalit stood up and gave an exaggerated performance of stretching lazily. He didn't look at Pradyumna who had transferred his stare from his guests to his wife. 'I think we should go, sweetie,' he said to Chanda, his voice breaking into a yawn. To no one in particular, he said, 'It's getting late.'

Padma sat holding her red salt-rimmed glass as they left. She waited for her husband to come back into the room, but he didn't. She heard him upstairs, opening and shutting doors and drawers.

Sandalwood

So I accepted the situation that my husband presented to me: after seventeen years of marriage, years during which I had stayed home in London to look after the children, he had discovered that he was homosexual. The timing couldn't have been better for everyone concerned. And if my husband had been a devious sort of person, I would even have called it manipulative; because his homosexual partner, the one who was to replace me in my own home, was a career man in a smart suit. He worked long hours. And so, how fortunate it was that the work of bringing up the children had already been done by me—Nidhi was sixteen and Pratik was fourteen. All they needed now, really, was for someone to feed them, and pay their fees, and not disturb the harmony of their social lives. The first of these things—the feeding—that imposter could do. I suppose I had better give him a name—it's Chandan. Though Chandan works full-time, my husband told me, I mustn't worry about the kids. Chandan cooks beautifully, has an eye for interiors, a taste for jazz, and an insistence on dust-free neatness. Thus, he would take over my duties smoothly; in effect, he would slip right into my skin at home and in bed. My husband didn't talk about the bed, of course, that was my own insertion.

It's not like I gave in easily. It's just that my husband told me every day, over six months, that my intransigence was ruining everyone's life. The children, he said, were living with a sword hanging over their heads ('You've already told them about this?' I gasped, horrified. 'No, but I'm tempted to expose you to them,' he said, 'for being so selfish'), he and his lover were in limbo ('Why can't you just have an affair with him,' I pleaded, 'why do you have to bring him into this house?' 'How dare you demean my love for him in that way,' he'd responded), and, he said, my own life was on hold till this situation could be resolved.

'What life of my own,' I demanded, weeping, 'I have given my entire life to looking after our family and home.'

'That's not my fault,' he said. 'I told you right at the beginning, when we arrived from India, to cultivate your own interests, make some friends, but no. You insisted on being a boring housewife with no personality, no taste, no hobbies but for your obsessive interest in your husband and children. And where has it got you? I've moved on, I've finally discovered who I really am. The children have moved on, you merely irritate them with your suffocating questions about what they've eaten and which friend they are chatting with online. Don't hold all of us back. Do the right thing and step aside, find your own place in the world.'

In short, six months of verbal battering turned me into a diminished person, unsure of myself, not trusting my own wishes, and, above all, not wanting to make things worse for my children by being difficult.

'I'm giving you a monthly maintenance, just for yourself,' my husband told me, when it came down to discussing the details of the separation. 'For the children, there will be the least disruption if they continue with me, in their current school.'

'Why wouldn't they go to their current school if they lived with me,' I'd asked. For all his bluster, I'd held on to the hope, till the end, that they would come with me.

'Because,' he said with avuncular patience, 'if they lived with you they would have to go to a cheaper school.'

'Then include the fees in the maintenance,' I said, 'and as for the rest, the children and I will manage.'

'Will you?' he said, tight-lipped. 'You'd better talk to Nidhi then.'

So I did. But Nidhi said, 'Mamma, Pratik and I want to stay here. In any case, we hardly see you during the week. I don't want to give up my room. Papa says if we live with you it will be in a small two-bedroom flat. How can I call my friends there? Where will I put my piano? Pratik also feels the same.'

I admired my daughter in that moment. She'll go far in this world, I thought.

So it was that I moved into a small, bare flat. It was only a short bus-ride away, but it was made clear by my husband that I ought to let everyone get on with their lives and not try to insinuate myself among them.

'Give it at least a year,' he said, in his most reasonable voice. 'A clean, sharp break for the children. Don't ruin things for them.'

I stuck to my daily morning schedule. I woke up at 6 a.m. I rode a bus to my old home and stood at a discreet distance across the road, watching the children get into the school bus. The first time I did that, Pratik waved. Nidhi looked furtively at me and nodded. Then she pulled at his arm and glanced at her friends to see if they had noticed the woman staring from across the street. The next day I didn't wave. But I knew that they knew I was there.

I had no job and no experience of working. The tattered half-life I led was one in which minutes seemed like hours, and an hour simply something invented to drive me to insanity. After the bus left, all semblance of routine disintegrated. But for the school bus, I wouldn't have left my bed. For weeks, breakfast before the bus was my only meal. Lunchtime would find me wandering the local park with a carton of orange juice in my hand to stave off thirst. By dinner time I would be lying in bed, staring at the ceiling and sobbing. What I did in the intervening hours I cannot say. Seventeen years were gone, gone at the first whiff of sandalwood, the damned whiff of Chandan who was now filling my husband's life with his odious fragrance.

Once, on a weekend, I positioned myself near the house to see what they were all up to, this new family. I saw them going off to some lunch party—new friends, no doubt—piling happy and eager into the Pajero, carrying a magnificent iced cake made by—who else—Chandan.

I never spied on them again.

That is, till I discovered that I still had the keys to the house buried in my purse.

At mid-morning on a Monday I let myself into the house. All was silent. I did a sort of inspection tour. There were plump new silk cushions on the sofa, making the place look rather opulent. In the kitchen Chandan had moved my prized knife set from its place near the hob. It now sparkled in a sunny spot by the window, next to a new pot of violets, making it look like something one would see in a magazine. I opened the fridge. Strawberry milk for Pratik, raisin bread for Nidhi, low cholesterol margarine for my husband, all was in order as it should be. Then upstairs to the bedroom. I expected my breath to catch when I went in there. But strangely, it didn't. It's not like we'd been active in the bedroom lately. I only cared for my home. I wanted it back, desperately. I want my things to be on my dressing table, I thought, as I stared down at the male colognes and hairbrushes near the gnarled mark on the wood that looked like a stack of pancakes. I want to cook for my children, I thought, staring at the tired face in the mirror.

When I left, I had a plan.

The next day, and the next, and the next, I escaped my dreary flat, and hung out at home. Why not? For at least a few hours a day, I went back to my normal life and activities. I tidied up in the children's rooms upstairs. I did a bit of ironing, taking care not to iron anything that belonged to Chandan. Some dusting. Useful things that nobody would notice. I watched television, made myself a light lunch. Chandan appeared to be a good housekeeper. But this house was none of his business. It was mine. Each day, after a short nap on the sofa, where I lay with one of our old novels from the bookshelf, I left the house at precisely 3 p.m. And I made sure that I left everything just as I'd found it.

But I started wondering what would happen if I made the kids a snack before I left. I missed feeding them. So I made some cheese toasties and put them on the kitchen island where the children always ate, perched on high stools.

Then I hid. I went into the store cupboard by the back door and peered out. I had an excellent view of half the kitchen. Right on time I heard the front door open. My children came into the kitchen. Pratik looked warily about him, but then sat down and ate. Nidhi looked at the cheese toasties, felt them with her finger, realized they were still warm, walked to the window and stared out. She appeared to be thinking. Then she walked back to the toasties and began to eat after dousing them in ketchup.

'Didi,' began Pratik.

'Shut up,' she said.

As the food disappeared into their mouths I felt as if a small black weight in my stomach was lifting. The next day I was in my element. I stitched on missing buttons of shirts and trousers, I sorted socks into pairs, I tidied Nidhi's wardrobe and sorted out Pratik's craft box. I vacuumed the top floor one day and the lower floor the next. And every day I prepared an after-school snack for my children and watched them eat it.

I began to find it odd, though, that they never talked about me. So just for one day I decided to skip the snack and watch for signs of distress. Some sign, any sign. But that day they simply looked at the empty kitchen island, helped themselves to some cookies, and went upstairs. I realized then how much they simply wanted a lack of disruption. That's all these children wanted. They didn't want me or need me. I was frightened at how little I meant to anyone.

As the days passed, and it became clear that the new family was doing just fine with or without my contributions to the housekeeping, I began to feel like a disembodied spirit, cravenly wandering about the empty house, a sneaky intruding presence, a ghost fixer of snacks. This house was mine and yet not mine.

Then came a day when I was so restless, I found myself making an enormous lasagne. I moved through my kitchen—with something remotely akin to joy, I suppose—mincing, chopping, baking, my agitation falling away. As a cheesy aroma wafted out from the oven, I began making pea soup, never once considering what I would do with all this food. In my mind I had even started on a cherry cake for dessert. I stopped myself just as it occurred to me that I was going to have to lug the lasagne back to my flat. Frustrated at having brought myself to a screeching halt, I began cleaning the kitchen. I scrubbed it to a state of divine glitter.

And then, instead of taking to the sofa, I fell onto the soft, duvet-covered bed in the guest bedroom and collapsed into sleep.

I hadn't slept so deeply in months. I had a dream: that the room had turned dark; and that there was a dark human shape sitting at the foot of the bed. I woke with a gasp in my throat—and found that it was indeed dark. To my horror, I could hear the faint clink of cutlery and glass. The dim red glow of a digital clock on the wall showed 8 p.m. My heart began banging against the walls of my chest, as if it would leap out and escape in terror.

I crept to the door, crouching low like a rat or some such vermin. I opened the door a crack. And I saw them all sitting around the table, ensconced in the yellow glow of the ceiling lamp. Eating dinner. To my amazement, the lasagne was on the table. They were eating it. Apparently, Brij and the children had no idea that they were eating the same lasagne I had made every other week for seventeen years. As I slowly backed away from the door, I heard the rustle of a piece of paper in my pocket. I fished it out. It was a note: *Don't make dinner again. I like cooking.*

Mili

I stared at my laptop, reading and re-reading the words. Mili was arriving in Bombay on the twenty-third of August. I think I was smiling broadly as I clicked the mail open. Even before my hand reached for the mouse, my mind was filled with luscious images of Mili, of days filled with conversations and hot chai, of moist nights and pulsing, never sated desire.

A short mail. She didn't give anything away.

Got your email address from Darius. Arriving this weekend for a couple of days. Are you free? Would be nice to meet. Mili.

Nice to meet? Nice? A word as bland as old bread. It meant nothing. Or it meant just that—nothing more than nice, but nothing less than nice either. But I understood her hesitancy, liked it even. She was checking out the scene. A too-friendly mail after five years of silence ran the risk of being met with mere politeness.

I fixed myself a shot of vodka and threw it back. It only intensified my desire to see her. I stood at the window, glass in hand, and looked out at the dark, breezy sea, marvelling at how the banalities of the everyday had overtaken my mind so completely as to make Mili disappear from my consciousness for five whole years, turn her into a mere passer-by in my life, someone I barely thought about. Because I now had Raima; her stories, her body, her love, had laid down layers over the past surely and steadily. It occurred to me, though, that it was convenient that Raima was away this week. I felt guilty, a scoundrel, when I recognized these thoughts. But Raima's presence would have complicated matters unnecessarily. I needed to see Mili alone. I needed to talk to her and move the ghosts out of the way before I introduced her to Raima.

Two days later, on a Saturday morning, we sat on the old wooden chairs of Café Mondegar in Colaba, sipping our drinks, the whirring fans beating at the warm air above us. Mili had walked in twenty minutes earlier, looking cool in blue jeans, smiling and waving as she spotted me. She strode confidently towards me, weaving her way through the other tables. A peck on the cheek. All the usual awkwardness of this kind of meeting. We spent some time arching our eyebrows, wearing overly wide smiles and exclaiming variations of 'It's been so long!' and 'You look really good!' But now that we had settled down and she had finished repeatedly running her fingers through her hair to smooth it down just the way she wanted it—I had forgotten she did that—we finally began talking like normal human beings. But there was one little detail that stopped me from being anywhere near normal with her. She looked beautiful. I couldn't take my eyes off her.

'I would have picked you up at the train station. You should have let me know which train it was,' I began.

'That's okay,' she trilled, 'I took a cab to Raul's, and his wife was at home so it worked out fine. I dropped my bag there and jumped into another taxi to come here.'

'Is that where you're staying?'

'Yup.'

I was looking straight into her eyes to stop myself from looking at the curves under her thin cotton top. She looked back at me with a steady gaze, a small smile on her light pink lips.

'And who is Raul again?'

'You don't know them.' She was the picture of poise. As ever.

'So what brings you to Bombay? You know it's great to see you.'

'I know. You told me that about three times already.' She was grinning, and I chuckled, delighted to be at the receiving end of her bluntness again. 'Nothing in particular brings me here. Just needed a break. I had a few days free, so here I am.'

I mulled over this little statement. Nothing in particular, she claimed, had brought her from Baroda to Bombay. She had dropped her luggage at this Raul's place and come straight to see me. And here she was. Suddenly, the weekend ahead lay open like a joyous empty canvas.

'I hear you're about to be married,' said Mili, smiling over her bendy straw. 'Congratulations!'

So she knew about Raima. 'Yeah, thanks. Raima. Her name's Raima. But she's away for a few days.'

'What a pity. I would have liked to meet her.'

I looked at Mili closely. Did she mean that? I felt like an opportunist, as if I had already cheated on Raima. But I couldn't help it.

I began on another thread. 'I expected you to show up wearing a khadi sari,' I joked. 'I hear you're into social work.'

She rolled her eyes, but it was in good humour. 'Oh please. We social workers can't wear jeans?'

I laughed. Laughter came easily to me that morning. Looking back, I think in some weird way it felt like foreplay.

'Just like you to say that!' she continued. 'When I first met you, you were hanging out in horrible faded kurtas and jeans and chappals, and I had the strongest urge to remind you that we weren't living in the 1970s. Even though Marx was your hero and even though you were a member of the students' union! Remember?'

Sure I remembered. The day we met, Mili had peeped into the student newspaper office. She looked bewitching, chic and slim in a clingy top, exuding the lazy confidence of the wealthy. She wanted to contribute a book review to the paper, agreeing with an author who advocated sops to laid-off textile mill workers—well-written, but I disagreed with it. We'd had a long and involved discussion.

'How could I forget,' I said. 'Remember that tirade I went off into on how workers have a right to work?'

'You were right, though,' she said.

'I was bang in the middle of my Marxist phase then,' I said, crunching on an ice cube. 'Did we actually publish that review in the end?'

Mili, sipping her lime soda, gave a long, exaggerated shrug.

As for me, I mainly remembered wanting to lean over and kiss those lips that afternoon in the newspaper office. Over the rest of our postgrad year Mili underwent a curious change. She usually disagreed with my political theories and ideological talk—it was all too radical for her taste. But she grew out of her penchant for action films and pointless shopping expeditions, and became involved with an organization that worked with the wives and daughters of factory workers. She said it was my convictions about social equality that got her interested. I'm so glad I came to Bombay to do my MA, she would say, I would never have got into this stuff if I'd stayed home in Baroda. And I would never have met you, she would add, kissing my eyes. By the time we were in the middle of our affair she had started talking about the 'empowerment of the poor'.

Meanwhile, I was losing interest in the subject. as graduation and thoughts of finding a job began to weigh heavily on my mind. After leaving university I steadily drifted away from the political jabbering and posturing I was so prone to as a scruffy student. I landed a hot creative job in an ad agency.

'Are you still at that ad agency you were always going on about towards the end of our final year?' she asked.

'Still there,' I grinned. 'And you, do you like what you do?'

'You know what I'd really like to do this weekend?' she said, giving me a mock frown. 'First of all, let's not talk about work. And second, I'd love to go to all the old haunts. See Bombay as a tourist again.'

'No problem,' I said eagerly, 'glad to be your tour guide.' She suddenly looked embarrassed, and I felt as if I'd been too intrusive. In fact, I spent a frantic few seconds cringing at the thought that I might have sounded as lustful as I felt. A delicate pink was creeping up her cheeks. But surely she'd want another taste of how great we had been together?

'That is, if you'd like me to,' I added hastily, 'I'm sure you have plans with your friends too.'

'I didn't mean to barge in on your weekend,' she interrupted, 'I'm sure *you* have plans too.'

'Actually, I don't. It would be great to spend the weekend together.'

She brightened and smiled. 'That's great. I'm having dinner with Raul and his wife tonight, but I told them I'd be gallivanting all day.'

So she'd already told them she'd be busy all day. There

certainly was a hint there that she had hoped to spend the day with me.

However, as the day progressed I became less and less sure of myself. We never spoke about our affair directly. In fact, we never spoke about it at all. The afternoon was spent zooming about in taxis from one place to another, chattering about old friends and old jokes. I started feeling a little uncomfortable. Sure, I would have jumped at the opportunity to make love to her, but now I also wanted to talk about us, what happened, why we broke up. Not that it made a difference now, but it seemed odd to spend so much time together without so much as a reference to the passion that had consumed us for a whole year only five years ago. Yesterday, five years had seemed a long time to me. Not today. By the late afternoon our endless jokey conversations, filled with clever puns and teasing repartee, began to grate.

Tired out, I suggested stopping by the Sea Lounge at the Taj for an evening drink overlooking the harbour before she left for her dinner. As we sank down in that chilled environment of hushed voices and plush olive carpets, weariness overwhelmed me. I didn't want to spend my entire time with Mili going from shop to shop, restaurant to restaurant, from one taxi to another, endlessly walking through ridiculous places like Marine Drive and Juhu Beach. When she said she wanted to go to all the old haunts she seemed to have meant it literally. I felt claustrophobic in the Sea Lounge, and, seeing an elegant stewardess already gliding towards us, irritated at the expensive efficiency of the place. But it would be stupid to suggest leaving when we had just arrived. I looked at Mili in frustration. She was patting her forehead with a tissue, perfectly at ease. Didn't she just want to talk? Talk about the old times, tell me about her life? I'd heard that she had got divorced a couple of years ago, but I'd been waiting for her to bring it up. As the stewardess approached, I remembered with relief that there was a small open-air section on the veranda. 'Let's sit outside,' I said, desperate to get out of the ice-box atmosphere.

'Yes, let's,' said Mili, looking pleased at the idea.

There was a restfulness in the cushioned cane armchairs outside, scattered amid tall potted plants. The air was now salty and cool, dinghies and boats bobbed peacefully in the darkening purple light down at the harbour and it was quiet, as if the hotel management had even managed to mute the road-life outside.

Mili sat sipping her gin and tonic, tired and still, and, for the first time that day, thoughtful.

'Mili,' I said quietly, 'what happened? Why did you leave him?'

She sat up. I had obviously hit a nerve.

'Clash of personalities,' she said, with exaggerated primness, as if quoting from a textbook on marital relations.

'Oh, come on, Mili.'

Her spine curved into the soft cushions again, and she shook her head. 'We were too different. Our views were too different,' she said, giving in.

'You didn't figure that out before you got married?'

'No. I'd only met him a few times before it was all arranged.'

This was unbelievable. 'You let that happen to you? An educated, enlightened woman?'

She laughed. 'Apparently not so educated and enlightened, after all. But I thought it might work.'

'And then?'

'I couldn't bear his witless life. So I left.'

'Why, what did he do?'

'He designed games for mobile phones.'

'So?'

'The more I got to know about it, the more it dawned on me what a frivolous occupation it was. Spending all your time convincing people to buy something they don't need. And I couldn't stand his obsession with office politics. Such trivialities when there are more important things to think about in the world.'

'Mili,' I said pointedly, 'I'm in advertising too.'

'I know,' she laughed again, 'I can't believe it. You of all people! And goodbye to Marx, here in the Sea Lounge!'

I suddenly felt angry with her. 'We can't all play at being poor,' I said. 'Some of us have to support ourselves, build a life.'

'I have to earn my living too,' she countered at once.

For a moment I wanted to shake her. Nobody who really has to earn their living would ever say that, I thought. At least not in that stupid, self-conscious way. I shook my head and stared out at the boats on the water.

'What?' she said.

'Okay, look,' I said, 'I know you're doing great work out there in the city slums. And Darius tells me you've spent the last few months working in a village near the city, which is pretty amazing. But just because you like to run off to villages in the fucking boonies, doesn't mean we all have to. Is that really why your marriage broke up?'

'I don't know,' she said. 'Maybe.'

'Yaar, just because half the country is fucked up doesn't mean that you have to pick up that burden and let it affect your personal relationships.'

'I know,' she said. 'I've started realizing that.' After a pause, she said, with a bitter smile, 'Shall I tell you something? I hate working in the slums. The desperation, the poverty, I hate it. The ignorance. Where do beauty and art fit in? Do they become irrelevant if you're poor and live in a slum?' She exhaled heavily, and lowered her chin to her chest. She began rolling her neck to stretch the muscles.

'Why don't you do something else then?' I asked.

'I might. It's not that easy. I can't.' She looked down, glum, and then glanced at me with humour in her eyes. 'You started me on this road, with all your talk about workers' rights. And look at you now.'

I looked at her curiously, forgetting to feel angry at the barb. There was a longing in her eyes, but I couldn't make out what for. Maybe she was living like a hermit and needed sex. But I was flailing like a fucking novice, as if we had no history together. My eagerness to hold her once more had disintegrated into confusion. But I knew what I thought about her slums.

'You, my girl, are on the biggest guilt trip in town,' I said, leaning back into the comfort of my chair. 'What do you mean you can't do something else?'

She gazed at me, looking hunted, haunted. I couldn't figure it out.

'Let's talk about something else,' she said, 'tell me about you.'

So we launched into more chit-chat, backtracking into the mode we had been in all day. For a moment she looked small, lost, the slightness of her frame exaggerated by the oversized armchair that half encircled her. I could hardly believe that she had spent five years working intensively in slums and villages. Somehow it didn't fit. She had lost none of her poise and elegance of dress. She could easily have passed off as a banker or a corporate executive. I could better imagine her coolly decked in diamonds than sleeping on a mat in a hut. Slowly, as fatigue set in, more than her words it was her face, the way she moved her mouth, all the familiar movements of her body, that began absorbing me.

She put off leaving me that evening till it was very late. Raul and his wife began to look more and more like an excuse. But if she had come to Bombay to see me, why was she not spending the entire evening with me too? Why the coyness, why, when we had bared ourselves to each other body and soul long ago, had we spent the day pretending otherwise?

The next morning we met once again at Café Mondegar. She turned up in a flowing white skirt, relaxed, mellow and ravishing, dark hair swinging loose and teasing her soft cheeks. Surely she must know how absolutely alluring she looks, I thought, and began wondering whether it was all for my benefit. No chain or necklace, her neck was bare and beautiful; thin, open sandals that simply and sexily revealed the shape and perfection of her small feet. Once again I had a hard time looking without showing it.

There was a certain new intimacy between us that morning. Only a few hours of the night had separated us. The fact that we had spent an entire day together and were to spend yet another in each other's company seemed to be of some import. An awareness of this undefined significance hung awkwardly between us. There was something about our mannerisms, our gestures, the way we looked at one another, that indicated a closeness, almost a proprietorship over each other. Only yesterday I had discovered that she had become a ginger tea addict, and already today I found myself exerting an authority bordering on the overfamiliar in ordering her tea 'with extra ginger'.

Already things we had said yesterday had been transformed into private jokes between us, little quips that no one else would understand. She knew I needed my shot of coffee every couple of hours; I knew that she had unsuccessfully looked for brown jeans the previous day; she knew that I needed to pick up a parcel from Churchgate at three o'clock; and we planned our day around these little intimate pieces of knowledge which, in just one day, we had gathered about each other.

Through the day, I thirstily drank in her company, her beauty, her scent, and was filled with recollections of times more carefree, more feverish, more simple. There was something about Mili. Something Raima hadn't yet given me.

That day our pace was slower, our talk less flippant. We browsed through the bric-a-brac stalls at Colaba, dawdled over a leisurely lunch. But I was not able to step past her reticence about us. I wanted to talk about us—about the hours we were spending together now. Conversation flowed in a way that made it impossible to even introduce the subject without appearing to be a bumbling bulldozer. But she did talk about her ex-husband as we wandered the hushed halls of the Jehangir Art Gallery. We'd taken refuge from the afternoon heat amid its cream walls and large blue canvases. Flat, car, job, a couple of foreign trips a year to look forward to. He was everything a woman could want, she supposed—but she wasn't that woman. She thought his bookshelf was vapid. He thought the books she brought with her were pretentious. He discussed politics with his male friends. When she interjected a contrary opinion of her own, his friends were embarrassed and immediately agreed with her. They were so very polite in those first weeks, she said, while her husband winked gratefully at them. Later they appeared impatient at her attempts to join in. Their wives looked surprised and a little hostile at the argumentative comments she directed at their husbands.

'It was a mistake on my part,' said Mili, 'to think I could settle down with him.'

'But didn't he know about the work you were doing?' I asked.

'Yes, of course. He liked the idea of a wife who did social work. But his view of social work didn't go beyond the giving of charity. He didn't think it would take hours and hours of my day.

He wasn't very interested in my views. It never occurred to me that he might not want a wife with opinions of her own, that it could be a drawback. I took it for granted that my views were at least worth discussing. How naive I was, na?'

'What do you expect with an arranged marriage, yaar,' I said. I felt exasperated. 'How on earth can you get to know each other within a few meetings?'

She looked at me. 'I really liked him. He was attractive, funny, confident. I had emerged from an intense project, months of hard work. I was looking for some fun. Unfortunately I mistook the fun we had together for something else.'

She walked to the centre of the quiet gallery, and looked around at the paintings on the walls. 'These are beautiful blues,' she said, 'makes me feel like going to the beach.' I was feeling pretty fagged out but she was so energized. So restless.

So we found ourselves on the beach at Chowpatty, strolling towards the sea. Some ragged boys were playing with a ball, their feet splashing in the sea whenever a small wave lapped the shore. A man clip-clopped by on his horse, looking for a customer to take on a ride. Mili began to look for pebbles to flip into the water. She made a pretty picture in the late afternoon sun, her long dark hair and white skirt stirring in the breeze, silhouetted against the sweeping blue-water arc of Queen's Necklace. She appeared to be standing in a golden pool of light. 'You should never have left Bombay,' I said, barely aware that my thoughts had turned into speech. 'Do you miss it?'

Continuing her search, she answered without looking up. 'Now there's a question.'

'Well, do you?'

'Sure I do.' But she still wouldn't look at me.

'What do you miss?'

'Lots. But none of it exists anymore.' My heart leaped. Surely—almost certainly—she was referring to our relationship.

'You mean—us?' I said.

'No. I mean me. I miss me.' Her tone was so peremptory— no, she did not mean us—that I felt horribly flustered. Like a fucking schoolboy trying to hold hands with the pretty girl, I had muffed it. But she appeared not to notice my discomfiture in the slightest and continued talking. She spoke as if she had thought this through often, and knew exactly what she wanted to say.

'You think I'm not in a relationship. But I am. I am in a relationship with this wretched city. I see ghosts of myself in all the old places. And I see how things intersect. This is how I was, this is how I am, this is how I'd like to be. These are the points where the past and present intersect. I miss the old me.'

'But you haven't changed at all,' I said, baffled at her melancholy. 'You're just the same— you're doing the same work, you even look the same, you're as beautiful and interesting as ever.'

'Thanks,' she said, smiling, 'for saying that. But that's the problem. The old me would have known how to move on, how to change. But you—you're good at moving on.'

She weighed a large pebble in her hand and threw it into the sea as hard as she could. It fell with an almighty splash. 'There I go!' she shouted, laughing. Then she began towing me towards a paani puri stall in a most resolute manner.

'No, Mili, no no no,' I said, shaking my head as I realized what the look on her face meant.

'Come on, you big sissy.'

'Mili, I'm not used to this anymore, yaar, you're going to kill me.'

'But I'm coming alive right now,' she grinned. 'Let's go.'

Back then we used to have Chilli Powder Championships and

she was determined to have one right now. So I rubbed my palms together and rolled my head, stretching my neck, hamming it up. We spent half an hour ordering the paani puri guy to up the chilli at every mouthful, gulping down cold Sprite, eyes watering and our mouths on fire. We each claimed to have beaten the other. Just like we used to.

'You've never had a Chilli Powder Championship with anyone else, have you?' She looked hopefully at me, her eyes still glistening with water.

'Nope,' I smiled, 'never.'

That night I took her to my apartment a couple of hours before her train was to leave. On the way we picked up her luggage from the flat of the mysterious Raul and his wife whom I still hadn't seen because she insisted I wait in the taxi while she brought her bag down.

She walked around the periphery of my living room, as if taking an inventory, and peered especially curiously at a photograph of Raima. I steered her to the balcony. As I set our drinks down, Mili's pure white dress and soft, clear skin, lit only by a dim lamp, stood out luminous against the night-blue sea. A steady breeze was picking up and she brushed her hair away from her face with a heart-stopping gesture. It was at precisely that moment that the thrill in my innards, which I had felt four days ago on reading her message, blazed up again and infused my body with heat.

'Don't leave,' I blurted out. Even I was taken by surprise at my words. Because suddenly I discovered that I was kicking myself for not taking the initiative. Like a fool I had spent the last two days in Mili's company without once making my move. To hell with the train, we could go inside and make love. 'Can't you stay a few more days?'

She glanced at me and there was no doubt that she understood the meaning of my question.

'Do you remember that night, Shantanu?'

The Banganga water tank. I looked at her silently, my heart thumping. We both knew the answer. Why was she asking me now? Did it mean she wanted it too?

'Do you remember, Shantanu,' she said fondly, steadily, 'how we used to meet for lunch, for coffee, for tea, how we endlessly tramped along Marine Drive to watch the waves at night, to watch the sunset in the evening, to feel the sticky salt on our faces. We met for a film, for dinner, for a silly boat ride to the Elephanta Caves where there was nothing to see.'

I smiled, remembering the blazing hot day at Elephanta and her pique at it.

'Excuses, excuses, any excuse to meet. How stupid we were. And then we had done everything that friends could do, said everything that friends could say. And so one night we found ourselves holding hands, and we walked from Chowpatty up to Malabar Hill, wandering, wandering, through the lovely leafy slopes, till we ended up there, at the tank.'

She closed her eyes and continued speaking softly. I watched her, fascinated, letting my eyes roam over her, as she leaned back in her chair and painted the past into our present, weaving one word into the next. She spoke with a frankness that was erotic, baring herself. This was a new Mili, I suddenly realized, confident, unrestrained, with the body of a woman, languorous, none of the pert, charming, girlish movements of the past. So here it is, I thought, we've reached the climax, the denouement, the real reason she's here. And I wanted her badly.

'It was so dark, so still. We sat on the stone steps facing the water, you a step higher than me, your arms wrapped around my shoulders, your breath in my ear, as if you were breathing only for me, as if no one else was really aware of the life in your body, the life that existed in your breath. I could feel your palms pressed into my skin, your body straining to hold back. And the silence between us passed from embarrassment into consent. We were no longer "just friends".'

She opened her eyes and looked at me. 'We never had been, I suppose. But now we were one minute away from becoming lovers. It was an unexpected moment. As such moments always are.'

She stopped for a while and then continued with her face to the night.

'I leaned back into you and closed my eyes. When I opened them your face was looking down into mine. Above was the black night, our own private canopy. Never had anyone been sexier, more desirable, never had there been a moment of romance like this one. I felt as if my entire life had been unravelling its plot to culminate in that moment, on those stone steps, on the banks of that old tank.'

She spoke fluently, as if to a rhythm. 'It was like the moment before dawn, when you look to the horizon and you realize that there is only one absolute, unstoppable certainty in the world. I felt so clear-eyed, as if I had never really seen the night before, as if I had crossed some line, gone through some ritual or initiation, beyond which colours, forms, shapes would ever after be more vivid, more real.

'I have never had another moment like that one,' she said to the sea. 'I'll remember it all my life. I'll regret it all my life.' She shrugged, and tried to laugh.

I stared at Mili, speechless at the depth of her feelings.

'Why will you regret it?' I asked, reaching for her. She pulled her wrist away when she felt me touch her, and simply looked down at the blank space left by the parting of our hands. 'Mili?'

'You changed me. I want to go back to being the way I was. Before I met you. But I can't.' She exhaled. 'Something is missing. I feel my soul is missing. I've left it somewhere.'

'Where?'

'Here. In Bombay. It's been nice. Breathing you in.'

I couldn't remember anyone ever saying anything more sensual to me. 'Mili,' I said, hesitantly, but it had to be said, 'are you still in love with me?'

She turned and looked at me.

'No,' she replied simply, 'I am not. But life has never been as good as it was when I was with you.'

I felt the heaviness of stone drop into my gut. Suddenly her arrival, her departure, her words, were all unbearable. I pitied her, and I was revolted at the degradation that my pity imposed on her.

She descended into silence. It was time to leave. The taxi sped through almost empty roads, for it was late. I hauled her suitcase out and we wound our way through the buzzing crowd of the train station. Finally, we stood in front of her carriage and looked at each other. We had ridden the taxi in silence for I was at a loss for words. But now something was pulsating in my mind. I felt that she was leaving without telling me everything. I didn't know what to say, what to do, how to pluck down those unsaid words hanging over us.

There was a sudden surge around us. People were leaping into their carriages, last-minute purchases of snacks and drinks in their hands. Down the length of the shuddering train, doors began slamming shut one after the other, and a voice began booming over the loudspeakers.

'Why did you come to see me, Mili?' I asked, desperate. 'Why now?'

'Will you believe me if I say I don't know?' she asked quietly.

A wretched desolation enveloped me in the midst of that heaving, steaming station.

'Anyway,' she continued, with tears in her eyes, 'does it matter?'

There was only one answer to that now. I held her fingers in mine for a moment, and then she was gone.

These Circuses That Sweep
Through the Landscape

I

The back of a person's head looks so vulnerable. Everyone looks like a buffoon from the back, slightly pathetic and clueless—the crown of the skull, the base of the cranium cradled on top of the spine—all exposed and witless. I am standing right behind him as he sits in his armchair. I raise my arms, hands clenched on my weapon. He does not move. He continues reading, head bent, the tips of his grey spectacle arms jutting out behind his big old ears.

Suddenly, I am contemptuous of this non-man. The instinct for survival, where is it? This is the point at which base animal instinct ought to take over, his head ought to whip around, his arm upraised to defend his face. Not that it would help him much. But it might make me respect him a little. Intellect might have helped him at one point. Even now, it could alert him—if it took the trouble of clicking into action, that is—that since I have not yet left the room, I must, given the layout of the study, be directly behind him.

Anyhow, here I am and about to strike. A house is full of possibilities of violence and murder. And I am not talking about the obvious potential of the kitchen. There are some pretty interesting things you could do with a screwdriver or a hot iron, say. A kitchen knife is convenient, no doubt, but maudlin. My choice of weapon is a hammer.

II

When the bell rang the old man did nothing. He just listened, wondering if it was the phone or the door. He decided it was the phone. He waited for it to stop ringing. But then it rang again. It now occurred to him that it was not normal for the phone to have such a short ring. Of course it was the door. He heard it open and then shut as the bell ringer was admitted into the house.

He shifted in his seat, ensconcing himself even more snugly in the comfort of his armchair. His life had been full of doorbells and telephones ringing. Always people wanting to talk to him, ask him questions, photograph him, bring him petitions and plans. It was all so tiresome because most people were fools.

There was a cobweb, or a shadow, or peeling paint in a corner high up where the wall met the ceiling. Did it matter what it was? Even if someone cleaned it, it would simply get cobwebby again. If he asked someone to paint it, he would probably die before the paint was dry. He heaved a sigh of satisfaction at the thought of his own death. There was something so miserable about it, and yet so certain that his thoughts returned to it again and again with a dreary fascination. But his preoccupation didn't last long. Within moments he had picked up a letter lying on the footstool before him, produced a pen, and started energetically scribbling notes in the margin.

The door behind him opened a crack and there was a soft knock. That, of course, would be Kumar, the official who had rung the doorbell just now. Or had that been someone else? No, it must be Kumar, he was already late.

'Kumar, this is my plan for renovating the School of Architecture. We have to refurbish it with a new arch and remove the stained-glass windows which are outdated and never get cleaned and, frankly, are a load of rubbish in this day and age.'

'Excuse me, sir,' said a respectful voice, 'I'm afraid I'm not... Sir, I am Kumar from the university... I had phoned you yesterday to confirm our appointment.'

'Eh?'

The old man wondered distractedly who this person was. As the information settled on his mind, light as dust, he continued scribbling, for there was a thought in his mind that he had to put down immediately. He looked up at the man standing before him.

'Kumar? Where are the plan papers?' he said.

His mouth twisted in anger when he saw the man was holding only a small diary. Get out and don't come back till you have the plan papers, he wanted to say.

'I'm here for the book idea,' the man said tentatively. 'I wasn't supposed to bring you a plan. Perhaps that was someone else?'

The old man sighed with impatience and said, 'Sit down, what is it?'

The man looked relieved, sat down and repeated everything he had just said, and added, 'I am from the Department of Fine Arts at the university.'

'Where is Kumar?' enquired the old man.

'I am Kumar, sir, but perhaps you are thinking of someone else?'

Then it all fell into place, how stupid of him. This was Kumar, the chap from the Fine Arts Department. He remembered the appointment now, though he had no idea what the man wanted. The official he was thinking of was called Sharma. Wasn't he supposed to come today, too?

The old man stared at Kumar. Couldn't be older than twenty.

'How old are you?' he asked, rudely.

'Thirty-two, sir.'

The old man looked sceptical.

'What is this book you are writing?'

'I have not started writing it yet,' said Kumar, 'it is a book idea, in fact.'

'An idea, eh?' said the old man. 'And what is this idea that brings you to me?'

He placed a cruel emphasis on the word 'idea'. But something boyish in the young man's face made him reflect on his own words. Why was he being cruel to this earnest young man? He answered his own question: because he was impatient. He didn't have time to meet every Tom, Dick and Harry before he died. Every day the letters came, every day. And of late they had increased.

Dear Sir,

On the joyful occasion of your eightieth birthday, may we submit to you that we would be most honoured if your gracious presence would grace our humble function for the benefit of the people of the country with whom you have stood shoulder to shoulder since the hallowed days of our independence.

Dear Sir,

Your illustrious name has been chosen by our esteemed panel for the Lifetime Achievement Award of the National

Citizen's Association, as the occasion of your eightieth birthday is an apt and joyful one.

Dear Mr Poonawala,
We would be pleased if you would accept the honorary Young Achievers Lifetime Award. Your presence would be an inspiration to our other Young Achievers awardees. Kindly contact us at the number or email below. Alternatively, if we do not hear from you, our awards representative will contact you within seven days.

How exhausting it all was. Though ancient celebrity did have its advantages, he thought, smug. He decided to play the old eccentric with this annoying young man.

'Who sent you?' he asked sourly.

'The head of the department, Mr Shevde, sir. In fact, sir, we have a separate publications department that produces books under the university imprint. And, sir, we would very much like to include an extensive profile of you in our centennial publication. Sir, it is provisionally entitled "Three Great Architects of Our Time".'

'I see,' said the old man, 'so I take it that you don't think I am the greatest architect of our time, like the rest of the country does, but only one of a group of three. And the other two are Padgaonkar and Khosla, I suppose? Both dead, so you can't catch them and present them with your idea, eh?'

The young man looked confused.

Good, thought the old man, let him sit there and stew. Damned Head of Department Shevde, sending me this half-baked youngster with his tired old idea. Poonawala, Padgaonkar and Khosla, the holy trinity of architecture in post-independence

India. God alone knew how many articles and books had banged on about it. And now here comes Shevde as if it's some brilliant new idea he's thought of.

'What do you want from me?' he enquired, brusquely.

'Sir, an interview at your convenience, your thoughts on the architecture of today, and perhaps some new reflections you might have about some of your own work,' replied Kumar eagerly. He had that tiresome deferential light in his eyes.

'Not interested, not interested,' said the old man, as if Kumar were no more than a door-to-door salesman. 'Tell your Mr Shevde that I don't have the time. In fact, you can tell him the truth—I'm not interested. I don't see the merit of your doing yet another interview with me,' he went on, warming up and becoming more petulant by the second, 'when so much has already been written and said on the subject.' His words faded into a mumble, and his chin sank a little on his chest. He was having trouble keeping his eyes open, it was the hour after lunch, when he was most like an old reptile on a sunny rock. The room was dark, however, and the darts of afternoon light that came through the thin white curtains spotted the gloom of the furniture with shifting puddles of yellow.

When he opened his eyes, the man called Kumar was gone. The chair opposite him was empty and the hands of the clock pointed to three o'clock. He had slept for over an hour. These days, whenever he woke and opened his eyes, when the familiar objects flickered into view, he felt a sense of evanescence. As if everything around him was no more than a shimmering, fanciful memory of what had once been. Many years ago, he had moved house. Now the thought of dying began to seem more and more to him like another moving of house. Not in the banal sense of moving from one realm to another, but in the strong sense of the impermanence of the present, the same certainty that the preoccupations and urgencies that had tied up that bundle of years and so engaged his energies here would be absurdly irrelevant from the moment of his departure; that these rooms would be filled by other bodies with other stories to play out.

Impending irrelevance—this filled him with a peculiar lethargy. Increasingly, it seemed to him that there was little point in the routine upkeep of order, just as there had been no point in doing so in the days before moving house. It mattered little if a corner was cobwebby or a drawer of papers chaotic. This kind of upkeep was little more than petty preparation for petty days ahead—a prudent tinkering and repairing of tracks for your little carriage as it trundled ahead—important in its own way, no doubt, for most of life was little more than small days and moments of no consequence. You were lucky if they added up to something in the end, if you managed to infuse the routine with moments of passion and creation, as he had managed to do. But now, at this moment in time, the time for petty preparation was long gone. He had little time left and there were other things to complete—'unfinished business', if he wanted to be dramatic. And why not? What else were his creations but manifestations of the dramatic?

He nodded off again.

When next he opened his eyes, emerging from the half-death of old sleep, the clock pointed to four. Punctually the edges of the white curtains commenced a muted billowing as a breeze sprang up.

'Janak!' he shouted, 'Ay Janak!'

Janak appeared with a tray of coffee and biscuits.

'Where's that man who was here?' he enquired peevishly, as if Janak were at fault for making the man vanish.

'He left a long time ago, sir,' was the respectful reply.

And where was Sharma, wondered the old man impatiently. But there was nothing to do but wait. Now the old man reflected on his recent visitor, especially the request he had made—'my thoughts on the architecture of today and perhaps some new reflections I might have about some of my own work'. A pedestrian request, albeit one that had not been made to him for a while. Indeed, it was so pedestrian and commonplace that only a man like Shevde would be tiresome enough to present it. But it made him want to smile, chuckle a bit even maybe, because it was precisely the question that had occupied his thoughts for months. He couldn't care less about the architecture of today. It was his own work he was concerned about—new reflections I might have about some of my own work. He certainly had some reflections. Though clearly, and irritatingly, he was being asked to 'reflect' because he was long in the tooth, as if old age were meant primarily for a meditative peering back into the past. Well, he was not made merely for reflecting, but for acting.

But to do what he wanted to do, he must wait for Sharma. There was something comical about the man. He was obsequious beyond belief. Comical and dangerous, the inner workings of the bureaucracy. How they all bowed and scraped before him, and how he played them like a grand piano. It was an accident that he was still alive. But they all hung onto his every word— when he chose to speak—as if he were an oracle. Apparently, his prodigious past had made him a seer of the future. Of late, the papers had begun a breathless dialogue about his eightieth birthday. How had they even known? He had stopped accepting social engagements a decade ago. He marvelled at this strange new capacity of the newspapers to manufacture and celebrate non-events. It was easy to generate glowing words, he thought contemptuously. Not so easy to do a serious critique of his work and analyse it. He felt grief—not a habitual visitant, but like a long-due neighbourly visit, it made its inevitable appearance now and then. Then he felt impatient again. Impatient with the world that seemed to survive on a whiff of perfume.

The doorbell rang. Finally, Sharma! The old man waited in the darkness of his study. He never ventured into the other parts of the house anymore. Here was a large, clawfooted desk, its burgundy leather top scuffed from years of use; next to it was the wingback armchair he was sitting in, odorous with his constant presence. The desk was cluttered with newspapers, books, loose-leaf paper, files. Tall shelves were crammed with books, and a wide glass-paned casement window looked out to the sea. In front of the window was a small round coffee table flanked by two Chippendale chairs. Dark, heavy wood dominated, sucking into itself the little light let in by the flapping curtains. Despite Janak's fastidiousness, an aura of dust remained in this room. A bedroom adjoined the study. But often, at night, he slept right there in his armchair. Now he leaned his head on the well-worn headrest and waited for the door to admit Sharma. A tall figure entered. The sun began its descent in a sudden blaze of light behind the man, turning him into a dark silhouette and blurring the details of his face. The newcomer sat down on the chair opposite.

'Mani?' said the old man in wonder. How long had it been—fifteen, twenty years? The man called Mani nodded. He looked at the old man with keen eyes.

'How are you keeping?' he asked, in a voice that was concerned and respectful, but not overly so.

'I'm still alive,' said the old man. Then he realized with disgust that he had said this with the mix of self-pity and humour peculiar to the old, and pulled himself up on his seat alertly.

He wondered why Mani was here.

'And you?' he asked, briskly.

'Also alive,' replied Mani, smiling, though coming from him the words sounded all right, like polite conversation. Well, he was a young man, after all. But as this thought appeared in his mind, he hesitated, as if something was wrong. 'How old are you, Mani?' he asked, confused.

'Me?' said Mani, leaning back comfortably, 'I'm sixty-five.'

'Sixty-five?' The old man began a tremulous smirk.

'What's the matter?' asked Mani.

'Here I was thinking of you as a young man, just as I used to,' rasped the old man, 'but you've caught up with me, finally, we are both old men.'

Mani joined him in the mild guffawing, for apparently he had understood the old man's train of thought.

Janak appeared with another tray. As Mani sat nibbling on his biscuits and sipping his coffee in silence, the old man felt discomfited. He examined his guest's scalp, found the hair was thinning, noticed that the spectacle lenses had thickened and the cheeks had sagged. But the shoulders were still broad, the stomach, lean under the loose kurta. Why was he here? He pondered his old friend's arrival. It made a strange sort of sense. Perhaps he really was about to die soon. Here he was, in the midst of planning his final architectural legacy that would, if all went well, mould his life's work into something new altogether, and suddenly here was Mani, also come to unravel knots from the past, no doubt. He hadn't thought that they needed unknotting. Well, since it mattered to Mani, he would play along; but at this thought, he grew crotchety. Why must he play along with anything at this age, he thought irritably, he was tired and he had a right to be tired.

'Who gave you this address?' enquired the old man, eventually.

'Shevde,' replied his guest.

The old man heard a muffled chuckle in his own throat. How tiresome Shevde was. He ought to be tied up in a sack and thrown into the Arabian Sea.

'What's this?' asked Mani, holding up a large drawing pad that was on the desk.

The old man squinted at it across the few feet that lay between them. It was a complicated doodle, a plan, in fact, a preliminary drawing for a plan, strongly scratched out with a black felt-tip pen. The dimensions of the roof, walls, door, floor, were neatly written in small, firm figures.

'Guess,' said the old man whimsically.

Mani frowned and looked closely at the drawing and its numbers. 'It's small,' he said, 'are you designing a shed or something?'

'Not a shed,' said the old man.

'Well, then it must be a bus stop, it's so small,' said Mani, 'but obviously it can't be that, so what on earth is it?'

'A whipping station,' said the old man, a shiver of triumph on his face, as he glanced at Mani in a crafty, sidelong way.

'A *whipping* station?' Mani looked dumbfounded.

'We need whipping stations in this country,' pronounced the old man, with the petulance of a thwarted child or a powerful dictator.

Mani looked at him and then down at the pad.

The old man felt a wave of ill humour. 'Of course it's just a doodle,' he said defensively.

Mani continued to stare at the drawing.

'Who on earth should be whipped here?' he asked.

'Vandals,' said the old man, grumpily. 'You weren't far off the mark when you said bus stops,' he continued, 'I've designed them to be as frequent and common as bus stops.'

'Why vandals?' asked Mani, puzzled.

'Mani,' said the old man, as if stating an obvious point to a dim-witted student, 'what is my legacy to this city, what are the main buildings that stand out above anything else that was built in the last fifty years?'

Mani shrugged, and said without hesitation, 'The School of Architecture, of course, and the National Library, and the Grand Palace Hotel, and the zoological society building, and the—'

'You can stop there,' said the old man, 'and tell me when was the last time anyone had a really good look at these buildings? They are obscured by commercial hoardings. My detail is defiled by posters for political parties, religious jugglers and sex films, and painted slogans about God knows what.' His voice was shaking with old age and anger. He was not used to speaking loudly these days. 'And they call it social awakening and economic progress,' he spat, 'they call it political organization of the masses, they call it the rise of popular culture against the grand edifices of the elite, they call it anything but vandalism, because calling it vandalism would necessitate some action. Flog the vandals,' he said, with sadistic pleasure in his voice.

Mani sat looking at him calmly.

'My architecture,' said the old man, trembling, 'is an architecture of ideas.'

'Great art is always about a great idea,' agreed Mani, 'it's the first lesson of art school.' The calm tone of his voice made the old man pause for a moment. Stubbornly he repeated, 'Flog them,' but then thought, nobody will ever be flogged for vandalism.

His guest seemed to know that the whole thing was just a

flight of fancy, for he had put the drawing pad back on the table and relaxed into his chair, looking around the room with mild interest.

'So what have you been doing with yourself?' asked the old man. He inhaled deeply as if new air would buff away the last traces of sentences spoken earlier.

Mani looked suspiciously at him. 'What do you mean?' he said.

'Just that,' the old man said. 'What have you been doing with yourself?'

'It's an interesting choice of words,' murmured Mani, and he repeated the old man's question. 'What have I been *doing* with myself?'

III

It's an interesting choice of words, I reflect. It's the sort of thing one might ask a housewife or a fresh graduate who's not yet sure what to do with his life. So, my dear, how have you been keeping yourself busy? Or perhaps it is his tone with its judgemental arrogance that makes me resentful. I too would have liked to be superior and paternalistic, to have been placed on a pedestal so that I could look down upon the world and say this is so, and that is so. And people would have listened to me the way they listen to this bastard, this 'greatest architect of our time'. What about Khosla and Padgaonkar, you might say. But compare the most average aspects of Poonawala's architecture with the finest of Khosla's and Padgaonkar's—and this old man still wins hands down. Anyone who can't see this knows nothing about architecture.

And it's true about the posters and graffiti disfiguring

his monumental, extraordinary buildings. But how curiously parochial his indignation is. As usual, he cares only about himself. Your buildings, I want to tell him, are not the only ones being defaced, there are others, too, which are being desecrated in this way. In fact, it is the entire landscape of this damned city that is being defaced. But I am startled by the sadistic streak in this old man that advocates flogging so vehemently. Whatever else Poonawala has been, whatever loathsome thing he has been, he has never been violent. So what is he doing, fantasizing about—I think I want to laugh—whipping stations? It is a useless design, this doodle of his, and yet intriguing, for I wonder what curves and waves of the mind would bring a great architect to this. To stop myself saying anything further about the drawing, I put it down and begin looking around the room with exaggerated interest. In fact, I am not in the least interested in the room. I feel his eyes looking me up and down. Yes, of course, I am old, I have caught up with him. I am filled with wonderment at his turn of phrase—'Here I was thinking of you as a young man, but you've caught up with me, we are both old men'. Quite so. He cannot claim the privileges of old age any more, not with me at any rate. Because I too have passed some invisible mark in time, and I too am old. No more the adoring twenty-five-year-old to his worldly forty. I feel slightly embarrassed at how fawning I was then.

Our eyes lock in a deep, appraising glance and I see he still, after forty years, remembers it. All this while, he is turning over the files in his brain to figure out why I'm here, like a clunking old computer. I am served coffee and biscuits. Nothing ever changes. I dislike coffee, but the great Poonawala only serves coffee in his house, his guests' tastes be damned. At one time I drank it unthinkingly, I would have drunk sea water if he'd offered it. Later, I thought this attitude exceptionally rude and arrogant. But now, since he is an old man, and Parsi at that, I suppose I ought to call it eccentric. So I pretend to sip my coffee and I chew on the same old Marie biscuits brought to me by the same old impassive Janak, amongst the same old shelves of books. Only the location of our meeting has changed.

Poonawala asks me how I got this address. I am happy to break the news to him that his address is not a state secret. How like him to puff himself up by assuming his whereabouts are known only to a select few.

'And what have you been doing with yourself?' he asks magisterially. What do you mean by that question, I ask him. I try to conceal my anger, and he knows exactly why, though his shrug is ever so innocent.

'I mean, what have you been doing with yourself?' he repeats, slyly. Well, I have news for him. I have a show coming up, my second solo show, a feather in my cap. How hollow and pathetic, though, that at the age of sixty-five, a second solo show is a triumph for me. But that is how it is, and I have learned to dress up my own small doings as victories. And so I bring out the same old phrases for Poonawala. I too puff myself up a bit.

IV

The old man looked curiously at his guest. It seemed childish for the man to be so proud about his show. He felt no small degree of contempt, for he set great store by self-knowledge. To have achieved no more than a second solo show by the age of sixty-five was rather pitiful. Certainly, put on your show by all means, he thought with a cranky, rather sarcastic, generosity, but surely you should be able to see that it doesn't amount to much? The old man felt disappointed. This was my protégé, he thought, for howsoever brief a period of time. But then he congratulated himself on the instinct that had made him lose interest in Mani. Clearly his potential had been illusory. He now felt embarrassed on behalf of the man who sat before him. He wished he would finish talking about his wretched show quickly.

'For the past five years I have been working on a project to translate the landscapes of classical Japanese art into photographic terms,' Mani was saying gravely. 'I have been trying to recreate the ukiyo-e aesthetic in my prints by using Indian landscapes of vastness and universalism populated with miniscule beings, not, obviously, as staged pieces but as spontaneous works of art, where I capture a landscape in its moment of truth where the landscape is everything and human lives but a tiny by-product of the indifference of its vastness.' He spoke in measured tones, using complicated turns of phrase and weighty pauses to show the old man that he was gathering his thoughts, so that it sounded like a commanding study of man and nature—all this the old man understood. He felt his eyeballs coated in a viscous substance, as if awakening from, or slipping into, deep sleep. But he nodded solemnly and said, 'Impressive.' Mani took another biscuit from the tray and sat back in his chair looking absurdly gratified.

'And has it been a successful collection?' enquired the old man.

'It hasn't opened yet,' Mani reminded him, 'but Saagar has been effusive in his praise and thinks it will do exceptionally well.'

'Saagar?' the old man repeated.

'Ramsaagar,' clarified Mani, 'of the National Gallery's annexe.'

'Oh yes, Ramsaagar,' said the old man , 'yes, I remember him, he always introduced himself as Saagar, the bounder, as if his real name wasn't good enough for him.'

'You know him, of course,' said Mani. The old man's chin sank into his chest.

V

As I speak, I am aware of my nauseating and reflexive desire to impress Poonawala, but I plough on regardless. I tell him that the photographs in this collection are a distillation of all that I have learned in my sixty-five years. Finally, I have found my pulse, myself, looking back at me from these landscapes. In this project, my thoughts and ideas have fallen into place, as if all my skills have at last been honed and perfected. I feel I can now build on this seminal bundle of ideas to achieve my artistic aims.

'And has it been a successful collection?' he enquires, after a pause.

'It hasn't opened yet,' I remind him, 'but Saagar was effusive in his praise and thinks it will do exceptionally well.'

'Saagar?' he repeats, confused.

'Ramsaagar,' I clarify, 'of the National Gallery's new annexe.'

'You know him, of course,' I say. Of course. Poonawala knows everybody and everybody knows him.

Poonawala's chin sinks into his chest without warning and I lean forward in alarm—what is the matter! But then a gentle snore emanates from him. This time, I can call him an old man without putting myself in the same bracket of antiquity. I do not fall asleep when talking to people. I do not spend my days in an armchair, as I suppose this man does. I feel a sense of healthful superiority.

I am at an advantage, at liberty to watch him sleep without his knowledge. I can unravel the man, speculate, through this visual stimulus, as to what is going on in his brain, I can peel the skin off his face as I regard him at leisure. But his skin is so old and moth-eaten that logic tells me it cannot possibly be peeled off smoothly, it is too fragile for that and would only hang in shreds. It would be like trying to peel a wizened old apple, you'd only end up with a spongy mess.

I now have ample time to reflect on the phenomenon of old age. Indeed, the room seems to demand it. It is silent like a chamber of meditation. The white curtains flap in the darkening air. An ancient clock ticks loudly. Poonawala is as immobile as a book on one of his shelves. Indeed, I feel I am the only living thing in this room of stultification and dust. This dried-up man with a bulbous nose, on which rest thick, grey-rimmed glasses, was once a person about whom it was said, in that old-fashioned way, that 'he cut a dashing figure'. With his talent and charm, he conjured up luck with a snap of his fingers.

And now he is going senile. It is a strong word to use. But what else am I to make of his recent perverse decisions? And so here I am, impelled to make my case, to tell him the blindingly obvious.

I lean back and stare at the moulding paint on the ceiling. I have obviously been in that attitude for longer than I thought, for suddenly I realize that Poonawala's eyes are alert and gazing at me like the yellow headlights of a charging car.

'Why are you here?' he asks.

VI

When the old man opened his eyes and saw his guest still sitting there, he decided he must get to the bottom of the whole business immediately.

'Well?' he said, 'what brings you here?'

'Your recent decisions...' began Mani, carefully. He seemed to be puzzling over how to proceed. Slowly, in the silence, a smile cracked open the old man's mottled mouth.

'Ha, ha, ha,' he guffawed, softly, 'so you've heard, I thought it hadn't gone public yet.'

'What I've heard,' said Mani, 'is that you have some plans for your buildings that will change them completely and utterly, which,' said Mani, agitated and blustering now, 'is, is, is, I don't know what to call it, is it a change of heart, or arrogance, or, or, what, is it, is it—'

'Senility?' finished the old man piercingly. His guest sat dumb and unsure.

'What I mean to say is,' began Mani again, 'and I think this may be very presumptuous of me because I don't know what thought processes have led you to this juncture, but at the risk of offending you I must question these decisions which, frankly, are outlandish and will destroy the basic fabric of your ideas, the beauty of your structures, it will be the death of your buildings, and frankly I find that almost, almost—'

'Blasphemous?' finished the old man again.

'Well, it would be an apt word, considering that you think you are God,' Mani shot back.

'Ah, but it is a point of debate, is it not, whether God can commit blasphemy—surely not,' said the old man, amused. 'Look here, my boy, you just tell me what you've heard.' Refreshed by sleep, he relished the pleasing sensation of intense concentration. He sat quite immobile, his fingertips steepled before his nose. Mani stared wordlessly at him. 'All right,' said the old man. 'You've heard that a music channel is sponsoring a competition for school children to decide the colour of the museum of zoology, is there something objectionable about that? It promotes an awareness of environmentalism,' he continued, in a light, sarcastic tone. 'In fact,' he spat, 'if I am not mistaken, the latest proposal was that the rear of the building will have an animal-themed mural painted by a contemporary artist chosen through a reality show.'

'The museum is a masterpiece,' replied Mani quietly, 'you built it to blend in with the old buildings in the area. It is part of the city's heritage. Why did you agree to this proposal?'

'It's a circus,' shrugged the old man, 'just one of these circuses that sweep through the landscape.'

'And what are you,' said Mani angrily, 'clown or ringmaster?'

'Ringmaster,' replied the old man smoothly. A feeling of fragmentation was suddenly enveloping him, as if he had already died and various parts of him had commenced a leisurely floating away. One of his eyes looked down from the ceiling at the two men seated in the fading light like a set piece from a long-ago, obscure production. Then he was back down, amidst the action.

'Anyway,' continued the old man, 'you can barely see the bloody thing through all the hoardings around it. What else have you heard? About the new extension to the Urban Works building? On the lawn to the right of its arched gateway?'

'And symmetry be damned?' Mani said.

VII

'And symmetry be damned?' I say. I can hardly believe what I am hearing. He is not senile, I see that now—so what is he on about?

'And the façade be damned too,' continues Poonawala, 'and also damn the eye-space and the lung-space.'

'What happened to the architecture of ideas?' I ask dryly.

'Going strong,' he replies, as if I were merely asking about his health over a genial cup of tea.

'That is to say,' he continues, 'I think the Urban Works building ought to reflect what the Urban Works Department believes in, don't you?' Now there is an ugly, ironical quality to his voice.

'So that's it? You're doing it out of spite?' I say, incredulous. 'Urban planning is in a mess so you are going to make it even messier by defacing your buildings?'

Poonawala looks disappointed. 'Is that all you think it is?' he enquires. A bar of late light appears pink and yellow on the carpet and instantly begins dissolving.

'It is very simple, Mani,' he says. 'This city does not deserve my work. My creations have been vandalized by our great democracy. My architecture of ideas only has a place in books. It has no place in reality. The question is, will I let my buildings go gently into the night? I will not.'

Poonawala sits in his armchair, august and imposing, as if on a throne. His words are persuasive like a prophet's. Prophet Poonawala. Suddenly it all falls into place, and I am consumed by jealousy. This needs some explanation, even to myself. It is laughable for me to be jealous of Poonawala, it is like a spark plug setting itself up as a rival to the sun. But Poonawala is not the sun that shines down on the world, he is a man like me. Only, life has offered him things denied to me. I have never been rid of the feeling that I might have been like him, given the right timing and luck. Many years ago, when Poonawala became too busy to entertain me and my devotion, and a hundred other things went wrong as well, I tried to kill myself. But, face-to-face with the tools of my death, I backed away. It didn't make sense, I told myself, because no one would notice. If I took my own life it had to at least be worth taking. And so I failed to die. And I tried hard to fail a little less at living. And now, even in this domain of suicide and darkness, which is my own, really, and nothing whatsoever to do with a man like Poonawala, even in this he has overtaken me, and he has converted it, like a magician, into a domain of light and action. Because the great Poonawala is about to pull off the biggest spectacle of all—the slow, public suicide of his buildings, his ideas. A suicide of his soul, and that too as public pageant. It is genius. And I gaze at him, hating this arrogant man, crushed by a pointless, clownish rivalry.

VIII

The old man had lived his real life within the confines of his own skull for a long time, and now, having revealed the reasoning behind his plans, he felt a little naked. It wasn't an entirely unpleasant feeling, however. He began feeling rather convivial, and wanted to ask Mani about his life, what he had been doing for the last so many years, apart from this infernal solo show of his. 'Whatever happened to that biography you were writing?' he enquired. 'Surely you didn't think the subject was not worth it?' And he made his eyes twinkle at Mani.

His guest shifted further back in his chair and gazed at the old man as if settling himself for a long chat. 'The biography remains unfinished,' he said, 'but obviously not for the reason you just mentioned. It was difficult to go on since you stopped giving me interviews.'

'Ah yes,' said the old man nodding. 'I remember now. It was just at the time the White Lily Hotel project came up. Wanted an entire luxury chain all over the country, the bounders,' he chuckled. 'Wouldn't let go till I agreed, but not that it hurt me, eh?'

'No,' said his guest, looking at the old man. 'It certainly

didn't hurt you.'

'I was away for months,' said the old man, enjoying the reminiscing. 'God Almighty, for months. Then they wanted one in Dubai, but I said enough is enough. They sent Zakaria to soften me up, and I thought, here we go on another round of dinners. It can get boring, you know, and how do you bloody well avoid it? But Zakaria came straight to the point. Clever man. "How much do you want," he said. And I said—here the old man paused dramatically—"*This* is how much I want." I was sure they would refuse. And Zakaria said—another dramatic pause—"'Cash or cheque?'"

Here the old man normally got appreciative laughter, which he now supplied himself. It was an old favourite among his after-dinner anecdotes, but he hadn't had occasion to use it for an age. Now, as he told it, he became a listener too, and found himself enjoying the story tremendously.

'And Zakaria flew out the same evening, didn't even buy me a drink, the bounder!' The old man finished expansively, conscious of entertaining and being entertained. Perhaps he ought to write an autobiography, he thought, it would read like a history of modern architecture, tell of a life of picaresque dimensions and poignant vignettes of an era, a memoir casually peopled by the great and the good.

He turned his attention to Mani again. He felt oddly talkative. He was too old to suffer fools for long, particularly new ones, but an old acquaintance was just the thing. He found himself envisioning future afternoon visits from Mani, not too often, but from time to time, when he could expound his views to his guest, talk about past times, not as teacher and student anymore, but as two old men conversing good-naturedly in the twilight, mulling over the ways of the world.

'Would it have made a difference if I had contacted you again?' said Mani.

'Eh?' said the old man, frowning, 'Contacted me again for what?'

'For the biography,' said Mani.

For heaven's sake, was he still talking about that, thought the old man. Aloud he said, a tad crabby: 'Perhaps not.'

'Why not?' enquired Mani, and the old man noticed that his eyes were unusually steady.

'There was the White Lily project, of course,' he said, 'and after that—'

'I know you were busy,' interrupted Mani, 'but that wasn't the real reason, was it?' His tone was combative, and it propelled the old man towards contempt, pity.

A man should not die without self-knowledge, he thought, and so he said, 'You're quite right, it was because I didn't think you would ever finish it. Architecture—or for that matter writing about it—was never your talent. It was truly unfortunate, given your interest, but yours was perhaps only a mediocre potential. Perhaps photography is your field, now that you say you enjoy it, but I wouldn't know about that.' There, he had washed his hands of the matter. He had said what Mani should have realized years ago, but the infinite capacity of lesser men for self-delusion was something he had encountered often in the course of his life. And to wrap up the matter once and for all, he said, 'Mani, passion does not an architect make.'

The old man was relieved when Mani did not respond. Now perhaps they could put the subject behind them. He hoped his guest wouldn't leave in a huff, for this evening he fancied company. The day was dark now, and the thought of spending the remainder of it alone did not appeal to him. 'Stay for dinner,' he heard himself say. 'Janak will be back late tonight, but we can manage,' he continued amiably, liking the idea better and better. 'I always have cold soup on his weekly evening off. You don't mind cold soup, do you?'

IX

No. I don't mind cold soup. I will certainly stay. I do, however, want you to fall asleep again prior to the cold soup. You have pulled my mediocrity into the light by giving it a name. I don't deserve to be called names at the age of sixty-five. So I will give you a name. You asshole. Name-calling is what you have reduced me to. It is the sum of my life, the computed total at the bottom, to be sitting here and listening to you pronounce judgement on my capabilities, my aspirations that you did nothing to help me realize. Here we go, your chin is drooping again, pathetically, and you have swooned away into an impotent la-la land.

The seed of what happens next has already germinated and sprouted shoots. I quietly leave the study. From the hall I climb the stairs and find myself facing a long corridor that stretches ahead of me and disappears around a corner. Everywhere there are closed doors. I am now in full control of the situation here because he is a decrepit old man and this is an empty house. My salaams to Janak and his weekly off. I make the rules now. I stride about unhindered in this mansion-like house with its high ceilings and heavy wooden furniture. I open wardrobes and drawers, deliberately rifling through old files and reading old letters, not because I am looking for anything in particular but simply because I want to violate Poonawala's privacy. It is a petty and delicious thing to do while I plan my next move, the important one.

And while my hands are busy with this task, I wonder where all the time has gone. I think all the way back as far as I remember, and a slow panic begins rising within me, for I find it difficult to produce an audit of my time, except in the vaguest terms. People spend their days creating a narrative to tell other people. 'From 1985 to 1997 I was an accountant in Bongman & Bangman. Then I did a part-time MBA and became a management executive. Then I was posted to Chennai where we started our family, and now I am a consultant in Bangalore and make frequent trips to the US.' They drape their lives around their jobs like draping a coat on a coat hanger; look, they say, here is my life, neatly ironed, creases in place, and everyone understands right away. Indeed, what's not to understand about a coat on a coat hanger? It is the main thing, really, one can hold it up like a trophy and people will applaud. But how am I to explain the formless, amoeba-like quality of my life, constantly dividing and sub-dividing myself to adapt to circumstances, forever reinventing myself—with my degree in architecture, my unfinished book, my camera, my pitiful second solo show. There is hate in me, and I direct it against Poonawala because he could have helped me and didn't, because he is what I wanted to be but couldn't be, because I loved him, while he thought of me as only a mediocre hanger-on.

As I open and shut doors to one room after another I am overtaken by the remarkable feeling that I am opening and shutting doors to different rooms in my mind. The entire house turns into a manifestation of my brain, with me wandering about in it. It makes me curious to find out what awaits me in the next room, and the next. For one thing, every room is cold and slightly draughty, which is exactly what the inside of my head feels like at the moment. For another thing, every room is empty and unused. There are odds and ends in there, certainly, but the purpose of them eludes me. A coat rack, though nobody uses a coat in this climate. A telephone in each room though these rooms are never accessed. An old-fashioned vacuum cleaner, brand new and still in its original box. An escalating sense of wretchedness and horror creates the buzz of beating blood in my ears. This is my mind, I think, unused objects, unopened boxes. Is it too late to open them, use them, is it? For a wild moment I experience a surge of energy and I think yes, yes, I can do it, I can accomplish the things I failed to do, I have untapped resources in my mind, ideas that have lain dormant for years because I only ever bothered to nudge them to see if they would awaken from their slumbers, but now I will prise them out of their shells, raise them to the light, fashion them into the extraordinary things they are, and the world will recognize me for it. Excitedly, I think of this or that old project that I could revive…but almost instantly the electrifying rush in my limbs ebbs away, and I feel fatigued thinking of the chain of actions that will be required of me, for they are projects that need the vigour of youth to complete them—to travel, meet people, apply for funding, spend long hours in libraries. I am left with a plunging sense of loss, forfeiture.

The time to set those ideas in motion has gone. I cannot use them now.

Then I come across a tool box. And I find something I certainly *can* use. Because the fact of the matter is that in this house that is a manifestation of my brain, I am conscious that the only room of import is, in fact, occupied by Prophet Poonawala. And I cannot stomach his existence in the only living, breathing space that exists in my brain. Let us see if he can prophesy what happens next.

I return to the study downstairs. Poonawala is awake and reading a newspaper.

'Where have you been?' he enquires in a gruff voice.

'I only went to the toilet upstairs,' I say, lying deftly.

'Upstairs?' says Poonawala with displeasure, 'but there is one down here.'

'I didn't know,' I say. He does not like the idea of me wandering about his house unsupervised, I can see. He cannot have been awake long, for he has not questioned the fact that for over an hour I have been flitting about like a spirit in the empty rooms upstairs, seething with rage and humiliation. He turns back to reading the newspaper and seems to forget my presence. I sit down on a chair near the window and think about how it is impossible to go off the tracks now. This train has started, I think, and it will only stop at the next station. I get up and casually stroll around the room till I am standing behind Poonawala, looking down at his balding head.

The back of a person's head looks so vulnerable. Everyone looks like a buffoon from the back, slightly pathetic and clueless—the crown of the skull, the base of the cranium cradled on top of the spine—all exposed and witless. I am standing right behind him as he sits in his armchair. I raise my arms, hands clenched on my weapon. He does not move. He continues reading, head bent, the tips of his grey spectacle arms jutting out behind his big old ears.

Suddenly, I am contemptuous of this non-man. The instinct for survival, where is it? This is the point at which base animal instinct ought to take over, his head ought to whip around, his arm upraised to defend his face. Not that it would help him much. But it might make me respect him a little. Intellect might have helped him at one point. Even now, it could alert him—if it took the trouble of clicking into action, that is—that since I have not yet left the room, I must, given the layout of the study, be directly behind him.

Anyhow, here I am and about to strike. A house is full of possibilities of violence and murder. And I am not talking about the obvious potential of the kitchen. There are some pretty interesting things you could do with a screwdriver or a hot iron, say. A kitchen knife is convenient, no doubt, but maudlin. My choice of weapon is a hammer.

I am gripping it with two hands. My arms are raised above my head, about to commence the arc of my downward swing.

Then Poonawala glances at the wall clock. 'Time...' he sputters, thinking hungrily, no doubt, about his cold soup. He begins to struggle up, his newspaper crackling in the crush of his fingers—I must act now, before he gets up. I feel a rush of hot blood in my head. My fingers tighten on the hammer, my eyes are fixed on his head, and as he shifts on his buttocks from side to side, I too shift my weight from one foot to another, like a woodcutter gauging the blow needed to tackle an old log. But then—Poonawala gives up. He gives up the effort and sinks back into his chair. He sighs. He huffs. He folds his newspaper in half and begins reading again.

This is good. This is better. Can I do it? Yes I can! And I lift the hammer a little higher over my head to gain momentum, to achieve a greater force to the blow...to delay a little, because I need to think. He's put me off with his fidgeting. I just need to breathe in deeply. Mindful breathing, I have done it before, I've done it at a meditation retreat. So, to focus my mind, I try to notice my breathing, be attentive to it, and I notice that I have, in fact, stopped breathing. So I inhale deeply, as quietly as possible. I pay heed to the breath entering my nostrils and descending down my windpipe to my lungs. There are balloon-like air sacs in my lungs; they transmit oxygen to the blood, and I exchange the oxygen for a lungful of carbon dioxide that I bring up and breathe into the atmosphere. But I digress. I am a procrastinating murderer. It's no good. I cannot even do this. Back to the business at hand. I grip the handle of the hammer ever tighter and I feel a rage crashing about my ears.

But before I can do anything, anything at all, Poonawala struggles up and out of his chair—he is surprisingly quick, as if reading a few more words has recharged his battery.

He pads towards the door of the study, opens it and steps outside, leaving it slightly ajar.

'Sharmaji is waiting outside,' I hear Janak say.

'Where are my files?' asks Poonawala.

'They are already in the car, sir.'

'Isn't it your weekly off today?' Poonawala sounds perplexed.

'That was yesterday, sir,' comes the polite reply.

I hear Poonawala's feet shuffling forward. 'Arre Janak, where is Mani saab?'

'Sir, he must have left some time back, you were alone when I came in to wake you up an hour ago.'

'All right,' he mutters, 'lock up properly, damned thieves might get in.'

'There are no thieves, sir,' says Janak deferentially, 'we will be back in two hours, sir, everything will be all right, sir.'

The door clicks shut.

I stand poised to strike, my raised arms frozen, like a warrior sculpted in marble.

Acknowledgements

I thank Aleph Book Company and my editor Pujitha Krishnan for being such a pleasure to work with.

I thank the members of the Bangkok Women's Writers Group for their brilliant critiques and all the insightful and fun discussions which helped no end in polishing and reworking many of these stories; members of the Yangon Writing Group for providing valuable feedback and keeping me on my toes; Prem Poddar for taking the time, over the years, to comment on my stories and being instrumental in getting my very first story published; Vasu Jain for always being encouraging about my writerly ambitions, and for putting me in touch with Aleph Book Company.

A million thanks go to my husband, Björn Rahm, for unconditionally believing in me and my writing life; and for being the invaluable reader and critic of first, and many subsequent, drafts. And last but not least, I thank the secret elixir behind all this: our daughter, Sukanya, who is actually a good fairy come to fill our lives with magic and sunshine.